To make peace with yourself you may have to give up a lot. You may have to give up feeling sorry for yourself, straining to be someone you are not, hiding the parts of yourself you fear are unacceptable, and worrying about what others think.

You may have to forgive yourself and others for not being perfect and stop expecting superhuman feats from your loved ones and co-workers. You may have to learn to accept parts of yourself you have been resenting your entire life. Indeed, you may have to grow to appreciate yourself exactly as you are and not as you wish you could be.

Why bother, or who cares, you might say. Your peace of mind, your love and work relationships, and your moment-to-moment vitality may be at stake. Making peace with yourself is a personal challenge that is certain to bring you enormous and lasting satisfaction.

Books authored and coauthored by
Harold H. Bloomfield, M.D.

TM: DISCOVERING INNER ENERGY AND
   OVERCOMING STRESS
HAPPINESS
THE HOLISTIC WAY TO HEALTH AND HAPPINESS
HOW TO ENJOY THE LOVE OF YOUR LIFE
HOW TO SURVIVE THE LOSS OF A LOVE
INNER JOY
LIFEMATES: THE LOVE FITNESS PROGRAM FOR
   A LASTING RELATIONSHIP
LOVE SECRETS FOR A LASTING RELATIONSHIP
MAKING PEACE IN YOUR STEPFAMILY
MAKING PEACE WITH YOUR PARENTS
MAKING PEACE WITH YOURSELF
SURVIVING, HEALING AND GROWING
THE POWER OF 5
HOW TO BE SAFE IN AN UNSAFE WORLD
TRANSCENDING
HOW TO HEAL DEPRESSION

Books authored and coauthored by Leonard Felder, Ph.D.

MAKING PEACE WITH YOUR PARENTS
MAKING PEACE WITH YOURSELF
A FRESH START: HOW TO LET GO OF
   EMOTIONAL BAGGAGE AND ENJOY LIFE
   AGAIN
WHEN A LOVED ONE IS ILL
DOES SOMEONE AT WORK TREAT YOU BADLY
THE TEN CHALLENGES

MAKING PEACE WITH YOURSELF

Formerly Titled:
THE ACHILLES SYNDROME

Turning Your Weaknesses Into Strengths

Harold H. Bloomfield, M.D.

with Leonard Felder, Ph.D.

BALLANTINE BOOKS • NEW YORK

Copyright © 1985 by Bloomfield Productions, Inc.

All rights reserved under International and Pan-American Copyright Conventions. Published in the United States of America by Ballantine Books, a division of Random House, Inc., New York, and simultaneously in Canada by Random House of Canada Limited, Toronto. Previously published as THE ACHILLES SYNDROME by Random House, Inc. in 1985.

http://www.randomhouse.com

Library of Congress Catalog Card Number: 96-96696

ISBN 0-345-41011-4

This edition published by arrangement with Random House, Inc.

Manufactured in the United States of America

First Ballantine Books Mass Market Edition: March 1986
First Ballantine Books Trade Edition: August 1996

10 9 8 7 6 5 4 3 2

For my dearly beloved wife, Sirah,
daughter, Shazara, mother, Fridl, and sister, Nora.

And to you, the reader,
with my love and appreciation.

Contents

Author's Note

To protect confidentiality, the names and identifying details in the case histories reported within the book have been changed. Any resemblance to persons living or dead is purely coincidental. Anyone with a history of psychiatric disorder or who feels emotionally unstable should not do the exercises in this book without first consulting a qualified mental health professional.

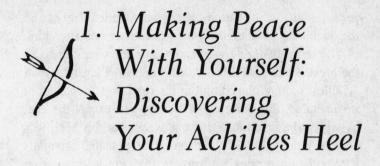

1. Making Peace With Yourself: Discovering Your Achilles Heel

If you could change at least one thing about yourself to make your life better, what would it be? What personal barrier has been your nemesis in your love relationships or career? If you asked your spouse, ex-spouse, close friend, or co-workers what your weak spot is, what might you hear?

We each have at least one Achilles Heel, a weakness, insecurity, or vulnerability that regularly trips us up but that is not a pathological state or deep-seated psychological problem. Indeed, people who insist they do not have an Achilles Heel are very likely to be the ones whose Achilles Heel is that they think they have to be perfect! Being perfect is not what this book is about. Only those characteristics that persistently get in our way need to be dealt with.

Most people will never seek psychotherapy because of their Achilles Heel, yet we all suffer from some vulnerabilities that impair our intimate relationships, careers, and personal fulfillment. Discovering your Achilles Heel can be the beginning of changing your weaknesses into strengths.

The term *Achilles Heel* comes from the Greek myth of the great warrior Achilles. According to the legend, when Achilles' mother dipped him in the river Styx to make him invulnerable, the water washed every part except the heel by which she held him. That one weak spot, his heel, was both the proof of his being human and his potential downfall. Rather than accepting his vulnerability and learning from it, Achilles defiantly sought to prove he was invincible. He repeatedly exposed himself to attack, winning several battles before his bitter rival Paris shot a fatal arrow into his heel.

An Achilles Heel refers to the part of ourselves that is both our greatest handicap and our greatest challenge. If we can accept and learn from our Achilles Heel, it can be a source of power, a stimulus to our growth, an essential part of our humanity. Yet, too often, we are like Achilles, resisting our vulnerabilities and forgetting our strengths.

> ✗. *We each have at least one Achilles Heel, a weakness, insecurity, or vulnerability that regularly trips us up.*

What You Resist Persists: The Achilles Syndrome

While we each have at least one weak spot or vulnerability, the question is what do we do with it? *The Achilles Syndrome is the price we pay for resisting our Achilles Heel.* If you try to ignore, suppress, or deny your Achilles Heel, it will have a tendency to reappear when you least expect it. "What you resist persists" is a powerful psychological principle. Even if you change your job or a major relationship, your Achilles Heel seems to follow you.

The "what you resist persists" phenomenon of the Achilles Syndrome can show up in various ways:

- Your Achilles Heel is a fear of being rejected in love and winding up alone, so you avoid getting too close to anyone or making an emotional commitment and, lo and behold, you wind up alone.

- Your Achilles Heel is your fear of losing your temper, so you avoid expressing your anger at minor irritations with your spouse, boss, or children until they pile up and you can't control your rage.

- Your Achilles Heel is your concern about your weight, so you promise yourself, "I'll be ready (for a new dress, a new job, a better relationship) after I lose ten pounds." Yet several diets later, after repeatedly losing and regaining the same ten pounds, your insecurities about your weight remain.

- Your Achilles Heel is feeling trapped in a less-than-perfect marriage. You stay together the first half of the marriage "for the children" and the second half of the marriage "because it's too late."

- Your Achilles Heel is a skin irritation that flares up when you are under stress. The more you resist dealing with the underlying causes of your stress, the more your skin breaks out; the more blemishes appear, the more stressed you become.

- Your Achilles Heel is your fear of "not being good enough" sexually or financially. Yet no matter how many sexual conquests you take to bed or how much money you accumulate, the need constantly to prove yourself remains. You can never be satisfied, either sexually or financially, as long as you are running from an Achilles Heel and doubting your self-worth.

"What you resist persists" is a powerful psychological principle. Even if you change your job or a major relationship, your Achilles Heel seems to follow you.

As a psychiatrist and seminar leader, I have encountered thousands of examples of otherwise healthy, intelligent, and successful individuals tying up their energy and creativity in the Achilles Syndrome. Resisting your Achilles Heel is like trying to drive with the brakes on. We are so accustomed to hiding, denying, or suppressing our Achilles Heel(s) that we don't even stop to ask ourselves, "What am I so afraid of?" or "Why do I pretend to be faultless and invincible?"

If I have discovered one thing in my personal and professional experience, it is how much we human beings fear each other. We're afraid of the judgments others make about us and afraid they'll discover the judgments we make about them. We feel isolated, as though no one can understand the insecurities or vulnerabilities we have. We're afraid to show any signs of weakness not only with strangers, which at times is appropriate, but also with those we love. Can you really confide in your parents, siblings, spouse, or children? Can you let yourself be open and vulnerable in an intimate relationship? Are you good at taking risks or admitting your imperfections? Are you able to accept and forgive your shortcomings and those of others?

What Is Your *Achilles Heel?*

Even normal, well-functioning people have some characteristics that keep them from reaching their full potential in their personal relationships and career. You may not know offhand what those elements are, but if you think back to those times when you felt hurt, angry, or unable to be creative and loving, in many instances your Achilles Heel was the problem. A good way to discover *your* Achilles Heel(s) is to carefully consider each of the following *except for*'s and *if only*'s:

- I generally feel good about myself except for_____
  _____.

- I feel proud of my body and appearance except for
  _____.

- I feel satisfied with my achievements in life except
  for_____
  _____.

- I avoid losing my temper except for_____
  _____.

- I'm usually in a pretty good mood except for_____
  _____.

- I'm usually not intimidated by people except for__
  _____.

- I feel I am easy to get along with except for_____
  _____.

- I have good common sense except for_____
_____.

- My marriage/love relationships would be more ful-
filling if only_____
_____.

- My sex life would be more satisfying if only_____
_____ ___.

- I'd be more successful if only_____
_____.

- I'd enjoy my family more if only_____
_____.

- I'd be able to slow down and stop trying so hard if
only_____
_____.

- I'd be able to deal with people more effectively if only
_____.

- I'd be a much happier person if only_____
_____.

- I'd feel my life had more meaning and purpose if only
_____.

If you think back to those times when you felt hurt, angry, or unable to be creative and loving, in many instances your Achilles Heel was the problem.

Over the past fifteen years working with clients and seminar participants, I have found that most of the responses to "What is *your* Achilles Heel?" fall into the following five major categories. See which responses ring true for you.

"I'm Afraid of Getting Hurt Again."

"I don't know if I'll ever find the right person."

"As soon as the relationship gets serious, I worry."

"I still feel very bitter about my divorce."

"Falling in love always seems to bring out the worst in me."

"I wonder if we argue too much/too little."

"I want to feel close, but I'm afraid."

"When I Look in the Mirror, I'm Never Quite Satisfied."

"I feel uncomfortable being seen in a bathing suit."

"When people say I have a pretty face, I assume they don't like the rest of my body."

"My skin has too many blemishes."

"I get embarrassed if my lover sees my jelly roll."

"I wish I were taller."

"My penis is too small."

"I wish I had a body like the ones I see at the health club."

"I Can't Stand Criticism."

"I'm always trying to please somebody."

"I'm allergic to advice, especially from my parents."

"I can't stand disapproval from someone I love."

"If someone's looking over my shoulder, I can't concentrate."

"All I want is to have my feelings understood."
"When my spouse is silent, I worry that I've done something wrong."

"I'm Always Feeling Tense and Rushed."

"I can't take a break until everything's just right."
"I'm always trying to do two or three things at once."
"I get furious when people don't keep their agreements."
"Between my job, kids, and husband, there's no time for me."
"I can't even relax when I'm on vacation."
"My mind never seems to stop worrying and churning."

"I Wish I Could Be Happier."

"No matter what I do, I'm never quite satisfied."
"I find myself asking, 'Is that all there is?'"
"I thought I'd be happier once I (got married, got divorced, found work, quit work, had kids, the kids were grown)."
"I keep looking for a way to channel my creative energies."
"I thought by now I'd have outgrown my insecurities."
"I'm a success at my work but wonder if my life makes a difference."

Now that you've identified your specific Achilles Heel(s), it's time to make a deeper assessment of the ways in which these constantly trip you up in your love life and career. For each statement below, check the responses that apply to you. Use the following questionnaire to see some of the ways in which your Achilles Heel runs you:

"I'm Afraid of Getting Hurt Again."

1. When your spouse/lover does something that reminds you of a painful incident from the past, do you

    a. Feel like instantly packing your bags and leaving?
    b. Stuff away your apprehension and hope it doesn't happen again?
    c. Discuss why you're upset and see how better to deal with situations like this in the future?

2. When you find yourself exceptionally attracted to someone, do you

    a. Invest them with mythological powers that make you feel tongue-tied and awkward?
    b. Search for a flaw or weakness so you can feel superior?
    c. Feel good about yourself in the other person's presence?

3. When your partner suggests moving in together, getting married, or having children, do you

    a. Feel suddenly claustrophobic as you stall and change the subject?
    b. Feel confused because at the same time that you want to get closer, you are also terrified?
    c. Talk about it openly to understand your feelings and bring you closer?

4. Once you have moved in, gotten married, or settled into a routine, do you

    a. "Get lazy" and take the other person for granted?
    b. Feel responsible for always making your partner happy?

    c. Find ways to keep growing as individuals and as a couple?

"When I Look in the Mirror, I'm Never Quite Satisfied."

5. When you first wake up in the morning, do you

    a. Frown and feel upset with the way you look?
    b. Look with scorn at your profile?
    c. Smile and feel ready to start the day?

6. When you undress in front of your spouse/lover, do you

    a. Get under the covers before you're seen?
    b. Make sarcastic comments about your inadequacies?
    c. Enjoy being nude?

7. When your spouse/lover looks at an attractive person, do you

    a. Wish you were better looking?
    b. Immediately feel pangs of jealousy and anger?
    c. Appreciate the other person's good looks without downgrading your own?

8. When you go shopping for clothes, do you

    a. Compare yourself with those who seem to look better in this year's fashions?
    b. Look for bland outfits that cover up your "weak spots"?
    c. Feel you are bringing out your best features?

"I Can't Stand Criticism."

9. When your spouse/lover gives unsolicited advice, do you

a. Pretend you're listening and automatically disregard the advice?
b. Become defensive?
c. Welcome your partner's suggestions?

10. When your children go out in public "looking like a mess," do you

a. Feel embarrassed that they're a reflection on you?
b. Hope they're mistaken for someone else's children?
c. Go about your business without worrying about it?

11. When you and your partner have a disagreement, do you

a. Try to make him/her feel guilty and wrong until you are "victorious"?
b. Give in for fear that this conflict could end the relationship?
c. Listen receptively to the other's point of view until a win-win solution can be found?

12. When you're making love and your partner says, "A little slower, please," or "Ouch, please be careful there," do you ever feel

a. Criticized as a lover—"I can't win with you, can I?"
b. That you must instantly stop and apologize?
c. Glad that your partner trusts you enough to be outspoken?

"I'm Always Feeling Tense and Rushed."

13. When you are about to finish a project, do you

    a. Spend hours and days putting it off or making changes?

    b. Wait until the last minute and work frantically to finish?

    c. Feel you've done your best?

14. If the meeting starts at 9:00, where are you at 8:59?

    a. "On the way" and frantic about being late?

    b. About fifteen minutes short of finishing what you need to have ready for the meeting?

    c. Casually entering the room and finding a comfortable seat?

15. When you set aside time for rest and relaxation with family or friends, do you

    a. Find yourself distracted by thoughts of work and other problems?

    b. Inevitably find your free time interrupted by unforeseen circumstances?

    c. Enjoy the time fully?

16. When you attempt to fall asleep at night, do you

    a. Have discussions in your head with people from your busy day?

    b. Worry about your plans for tomorrow?

    c. Feel complete and relaxed as you drift off to sleep?

"I Wish I Could Be Happier."

17. When you think about your primary love relationship, do you

    a. Fantasize about how much better your life would

be if only you got married, got divorced, were with someone else?

b. Worry that you can't continue to settle for less than an ideal situation?

c. Feel good about your relationship?

18. When you think about your career and accomplishments, do you

    a. Undervalue your successes and plague yourself with thoughts of what you could have done differently?

    b. Regret that you never risked living up to your fullest potential?

    c. Feel proud of your past and optimistic about your future?

19. When you are faced with loss or frustration, do you

    a. Catastrophize and feel life isn't worth living?

    b. Feel overwhelmed by guilt or second-guessing?

    c. Deal compassionately and effectively with life's ups and downs?

20. When you think about your own happiness, do you

    a. Fear your happiness or good times won't last?

    b. Wonder if you've been "faking it" to appear happier than you really are?

    c. Consider yourself an exciting and fulfilled human being?

If in this questionnaire you found yourself checking off lots of *a*'s and *b*'s, welcome to the club! These Achilles Heels seem to plague us all. Looking back over the ones you checked, which responses had the biggest emotional charge for you? Which revealed a pattern or issue that has been repetitive in your life? Which responses reminded you of someone close to you? Several of the Achilles Heels may not trouble you but may disturb someone you love or work with and therefore intimately effect you.

The rest of the book will help you to master your specific Achilles Heel(s). Here are several important principles that are necessary for you to deal with any Achilles Heel more effectively:

You Are Bigger than Your Achilles Heel

The irony of an Achilles Heel is that Achilles' five-foot-eight-inch body had only three inches of weakness, and yet those three inches became his downfall. Like Achilles, many of us view our weaknesses as if they are the sole measure of our attractiveness and self-worth. Rather than appreciating ourselves as essentially whole and good, we let our insecurities convince us that those "three inches" (of hairline, waistline, or emotional hypersensitivity) are more important than the whole of our body, mind, and spirit. Instead of seeing our Achilles Heel in its proper perspective, we fear it is a shameful flaw we must hide from ourselves and others. Soon our life becomes a losing battle to make up for our shortcomings rather than improving on an already worthy foundation.

When you see your Achilles Heel as a much larger barrier or problem than it really is, you are in effect hating yourself for what amounts to, by analogy, no more than three inches on a five-foot-eight-inch frame. For example, Janet's Achilles Heel is her fear that the lines on her face make her look older than her years. Ask her if she worries about turning fifty and she'll joke about vintage wines getting better with age. Only when you begin to probe deeper does it become apparent how much of her self-image Janet has tied up with her wrinkles.

As with any Achilles Heel, Janet's problem is not the lines on her face but her attitude about them. She feels uncomfortable when a man sees her without makeup. She fears looking older and less attractive than her friends and co-workers. Janet thinks twice whenever she sees an advertisement for lotions, clinics, or even surgical remedies that promise her everything from restored youth to more sex appeal. By accepting the double standard of society—that lines on a man's face make him more handsome and distinguished, whereas lines on a woman's face are to be dreaded—Janet underestimates her own good looks and vitality.

Another example is Karl, whose Achilles Heel is his intolerance of other people's mistakes. Karl is the kind of boss who is constantly looking over his employees' shoulders and finding fault. His wife and children also fear his quick temper and demanding nature. In a self-fulfilling prophecy, Karl's Achilles Heel actually increases the foul-ups at work and at home. His edginess makes those around him more error-prone and dissatisfied.

Instead of being defensive about his critical nature, Karl needs to learn to become bigger than his Achilles Heel. *All growth is the integration of seemingly opposite values*: Karl needs to balance his perfectionism with greater patience and understanding for himself as well as for those around him. He must not only set high standards but also learn to give equally high amounts of guidance and appreciation. Instead of focusing so much on mistakes, Karl could experience less frustration and get better results by catching others doing something right.

> ✗ *All growth is the integration of seemingly opposite values.*

Deficiency Versus Growth Edge

An Achilles Heel can be seen from two very different perspectives. Most of us start with a sense of irritation and frustration that we aren't living up to our own or someone else's standard of perfection. We berate ourselves with comments like "How could I be so stupid?" or "I just can't seem to do anything right." This attitude that an Achilles Heel is a *deficiency* stems from a basic perception that we are flawed. It implies that you are "defective" and unworthy because of your shortcomings. It views your Achilles Heel as something terrible you must get rid of if you are ever to be happy.

The other way to view your Achilles Heel is to see yourself as basically intelligent, loving, and worthwhile, including several *growth edges* that make life interesting. Operating from this growth-edge perspective, you can improve yourself without beating yourself up in the process. You can reach challenging goals without feeling as though your entire self-worth depends on whether you get rid of your weak spots. Seeing your Achilles Heel as a growth edge means working from where you are rather than wishing you were somehow different. Viewing your insecurities as growth opportunities helps you remember that you are bigger than your Achilles Heel.

The challenge of any Achilles Heel is to learn to *appreciate yourself exactly as you are, including your weak spots and vulnerabilities*. Instead of tying up your energy in self-hate and criticism, you will then be free to support yourself in learning new habits.

For example, if you have been trying to lose weight because you can't stand the way you look and hate yourself every time you get on the scale, any weight loss will inevitably be short-lived. A week or a month later the pounds will be back. If your diet routine consists of starving yourself one week and then binge-eating the next, you cannot possibly develop the habits of pleasurable, sustained weight control.

Regardless of what your Achilles Heel may be, loving yourself with a balance of acceptance and self-discipline is a key to achieving mastery. By "accepting your Achilles Heel" I do not mean you should become complacent or lazy. Nor am I suggesting that you must settle for something unhealthy or dissatisfying. I raise this issue of self-acceptance to make sure you don't fall into the common trap of lamenting or blindly rebelling against your Achilles Heel(s).

What you put your attention on in life grows stronger. If you see your Achilles Heel as a shameful flaw, you will treat it as such and encourage others to treat it the same way. You will be apologizing for your "deficiency" when an apology isn't necessary, or else criticizing yourself when encouragement and support are what are needed. Rather than resisting your Achilles Heel, you are being asked to identify your growth edge in order to raise your self-image, master your most persistent personal barriers, and increase your satisfaction.

> ✗ *You have to appreciate yourself exactly as you are, including your weak spots and vulnerabilities, as a basis for lasting change.*

Your Achilles Heel: An Opportunity for Growth

Far from being an obstacle, your Achilles Heel can serve as an opportunity for improving your life. Yet in overcoming any personal barrier there is always some bad news along with the good. The bad news is that your Achilles Heel may never completely disappear. A chronic worrier, pleaser, or overachiever, just like a compulsive drinker, smoker, or gambler, may have some urges and temptations to deal with long after he or she has been "cured." A person who fears failure, uncertainty, or other people's anger doesn't miraculously become fearless overnight. There is a natural tendency to revert to form under stress. When you are anxious, rushed, or fatigued, bad habits you thought were eliminated may, even for a moment, return.

The good news is that by discovering your Achilles Heel and coming to grips with it, you can make your self-defeating behavior less automatic, less resistant to change, and much more quickly resolved. Your Achilles Heel will become an important early warning signal that something needs attention within yourself, your love relationships, or your career.

Instead of reacting in anger or frustration when you notice your Achilles Heel, you will be able to ask yourself, "What can I learn from this situation?" and "How can I turn my apparent vulnerability into a source of greater strength, compassion, and well-being?"

Most growth takes place in a spiral, not a straight line; we tend to take two steps forward and one back. Instead of getting down on yourself each time your Achilles Heel reappears or your growth is temporarily sidetracked, those are the times to give yourself added support and guidance. Rather than continuing to be your own worst critic, you will learn how to nurture and coach yourself through difficult challenges.

While I will not attempt to cover every Achilles Heel under the sun, the strategies and techniques developed for each of the five most common types of Achilles Heels will help you master any recurring weakness you may have. The exercises and insights will not only help you be more aware of what tends to trip *you* up, but also make you more effective in dealing with the Achilles Heels of your mate, children, friends, and co-workers.

The remaining chapters are like personal counseling sessions, which emphasize that *all growth is a combination of both insight and behavior change*. Insight without change can be frustrating. For growth, one must also take specific steps to help break the self-defeating patterns of the Achilles Syndrome. Easy-to-follow exercises will show you how to transform your Achilles Heel into a powerful opportunity for growth. Illustrative case histories and practical guidelines will demonstrate obstacles that may arise and how to overcome them.

To make peace with yourself, you may have to give up a lot. You may have to give up feeling sorry for yourself, straining to be someone you are not, hiding the parts of yourself you fear are unacceptable, and worrying about what others might think. You may have to forgive yourself and others for not being perfect and stop expecting superhuman feats from your loved ones and co-workers. You may have to learn to accept parts of yourself you have been resenting your entire life. Indeed, you may have to grow to appreciate yourself exactly as you are and not as you wish you could be.

Why bother, or who cares, you might say? Why not continue to spend the rest of your life settling for less than your potential? Making peace with yourself is a gift you deserve for being courageous enough to admit that to be alive is to be vulnerable. Your peace of mind, your love and work relationships, and your moment-to-moment vitality may be at stake. Choosing between the self-defeating resistance of Achilles and the full expression of your uniqueness is up to you. Making peace with yourself is a personal challenge that is certain to bring you enormous and lasting satisfaction.

2. Making Peace With Your Past: "I'm Afraid of Getting Hurt Again"

We all need to love and be loved, yet finding and sustaining an intimate relationship can be one of life's most difficult challenges. This may be the result of painful childhood experiences. It may also come about if we have been hurt or rejected in our adult love relationships so that we're afraid to risk again. If we have fallen in love only to be bitterly disappointed, we may question our own judgment. If we have sacrificed to make our partner happy only to feel taken for granted, we may wonder if intimacy is worth the sacrifice.

When a love relationship fails to live up to expectations, our protective shell may thicken. Though we long to be appreciated, nurtured, and loved, guarding our affection too closely creates a vicious cycle. The more we resist being open and vulnerable, the more loneliness and frustration persist. The fear of getting hurt blocks our love and keeps

21

us from a secure and lasting intimacy. It may be the most painful Achilles Heel.

> ✗. *The more we resist being open and vulnerable, the more loneliness and frustration persist. The fear of getting hurt blocks our love and keeps us from a secure and lasting intimacy.*

One of the saddest things I see in my professional career is the harm people do to themselves and to each other trying to guard against becoming too vulnerable. Every day I hear individuals and couples longing to share greater intimacy, yet unable to because of a fear of getting hurt. Whether you are married, divorced, looking for a new relationship, or wanting to get out of one, there are easily recognizable signs you may be suffering from the Achilles Heel that we call "I'm afraid of getting hurt again." Which of the following apply to you?

- "When I get intimately involved, my common sense flies out the window."

- "I worry that my partner will get tired of me."

- "Relationships seem to bring out the worst in me."

- "I'm afraid my career would suffer if I made a commitment to settle down."

- "As soon as it starts to get serious, my doubts appear."

- "Everyone I'm attracted to is either married, in love with someone else, or somehow unavailable."

- "I'm giving too much and getting too little in return."

- "I've been on my own for so long, I couldn't live with someone else."

- "I'm afraid of falling into the same kind of unhappy marriage my parents had."

- "After what I went through with my ex, I'll never be able to trust anyone."

- "I worry that there's something missing in our relationship."

- "No one will ever be able to replace my wife (or husband) who died."

To protect yourself against further disappointment, you tell yourself, "I'll just date." Yet before you know it, the person you're "just dating" wants to get serious, move in, or talk about marriage, and the dilemma hits you once again. Should you settle for someone less than Mr. or Ms. Right? You may wonder if you're only staying with your current lover because the situation is secure and familiar. Sometimes you think you should find someone better but are afraid of winding up alone or with someone worse.

If you are tired of discovering "There's something wrong with everyone I fall in love with," there are a few possibilities to consider. Perhaps, because of your circumstances, you have the chance to meet very few people and therefore are entering relationships you know from the start won't work. Perhaps you have a need to choose the wrong candidates. Perhaps you are setting up potentially fine candidates to do something to disappoint you. In these cases you can then feel justified saying, "See, I told you they're all the same."

"I Keep Finding the Wrong Person"

Many people tend to fall in love with someone who can't form a long-term committed relationship—for example, they become romantically attached to the perennial married man who always implies that he is getting a divorce. A likely candidate for marriage or heartache? You decide. Sometimes, therefore, a fear of getting hurt is not just a psychological hazard to be dismissed or overcome. With certain people your reservations and reluctance may be entirely correct, and your fear may be signaling you to make contact with your better judgment.

One of the paradoxes of love is that we may be attracted to people with characteristics we later become repelled by. Some common examples are the following:

- You choose an insecure person for a partner knowing he or she won't leave you, but later find this person so insecure you're claustrophobic and want to leave yourself.

- You find yourself fascinated by someone who has a sharp tongue or incredible wit, only to resent later being a constant butt of his or her insensitive jokes and verbal attacks.

- You like someone with whom you feel comfortable, only to find that familiarity breeds first boredom, then contempt.

- You find someone who seems instantly intimate and incredible in bed, but with time discover this person is terrified of genuine feelings and closeness.

- You are attracted to someone who is defiant and "challenging," only to find that this person's hostility is now directed at you.

- You are easy prey for the expert seducer and you are fascinated by his or her ability to fulfill all your desires continually. However, over time you discover your partner needs to practice these "expert seducer" skills on the next "love 'em and leave 'em" victim.

> ✍ *One of the paradoxes of love is that we may be attracted to people with characteristics we later become repelled by.*

The most common symptom of this Achilles Heel is choosing partners who remind us of a difficult parent. When you have unfinished business with a parent, you may at times experience with your love partner the same feelings of guilt, hurt, anger, rage, or entrapment you felt as a child. If your father was dictatorial or belittling, you may find yourself attracted to someone who is either too much like your father or so much the opposite that you later resent this person for being too meek or compliant. If your mother was overbearing or made you feel guilty, you may feel enraged whenever your partner expresses a need or makes a request of you. If a parent was cold and withheld affection, you may find yourself attracted to and later enraged by the cold aloofness of your partner. If a parent died or emotionally abandoned you when you were young, you may be subconsciously fearing your adult love partner might do the same.

One of Sigmund Freud's discoveries that will stand the test of time is the repetition compulsion, that whatever is incomplete from the past we tend to re-create. Since some unresolved hurts will be retriggered by any intimate partnership, the key is to deal with these feelings *without* destroying the relationship. Only if you recognize that this slush fund of anger is directed toward your parents and not your current partner can you avoid letting these past hurts turn you against your lover. You don't need to leave a good relationship simply because your partner has restimulated these painful memories. To the contrary, if you learn to work through the unresolved hurts from the past, you and your partner can grow much closer.

> ⟍ *When you have unfinished business with a parent, you may at times experience with your love partner the same feelings of guilt, hurt, anger, rage, or entrapment you felt as a child.*

As I describe in detail in my previous book, *Making Peace With Your Parents,** cleaning up unfinished business

---

*By Harold H. Bloomfield, M.D., with Leonard Felder, Ph.D. (New York: Random House, 1983).

with your parents is one of the greatest gifts you can give yourself, your love partner and children. Learning to forgive your parents is not just for their benefit but for you, for your peace of mind and the quality of all your adult relationships.

In addition to unresolved hurts from the past, you may be carrying unrealistic judgments and expectations into your romantic relationships. If one or both parents catered to your every whim and need, you might be expecting your adult partner to live up to an impossible standard. If you were repeatedly told, "Don't settle for anything less," you may become disenchanted with every potential partner you're attracted to. If your parents fought either too much or not at all, you may have unrealistic notions about whether and how often you and your partner should argue. It's impossible to evaluate your partner or relationship accurately when your vision is colored by these expectations and judgments.

"If You Truly Loved Me, You Would . . ."

Marcie's case demonstrates how to identify and overcome the judgments and expectations that can undermine your ability to sustain a quality love relationship. A successful advertising executive, Marcie recently turned thirty-four and became increasingly concerned about her ticking biological clock. As she described it, "I want to get married and have children but seem to keep finding the wrong person. I've been in several relationships where I thought, 'This is *it*.' Yet after six months or a year I get this nagging feeling I've picked another loser."

Marcie and her current lover, Victor, a graphic artist who does business with Marcie's agency, have been seeing each other regularly for almost a year. When Victor suggested they move in together, Marcie's feelings began to change. She recalls, "All sorts of things I used to ignore suddenly became important: He's a night person and I'm an early riser; he's shorter than me when I wear heels; he orders the house wine without even knowing if it's any good. I love Victor but I don't want to make a mistake."

As I explained to Marcie, the way this Achilles Heel functions is that the closer we come to making a commitment, the more fears and doubts arise. Invariably, we can find good reasons to either split or make a go of it. Part of becoming less judgmental is accepting that we all make judgments; the less you resist the fact that no partner will ever fit all your pictures, the more you can appreciate whomever you are with.

Some judgments, of course, *are* appropriate. If your partner has a history of drug abuse, of always being unfaithful, of never being able to make a living, you would be right to be cautious.

In most cases, however, it helps simply to acknowledge the things you think are less than perfect about your partner without trying to deny your judgments or expect the other person to change miraculously overnight. The following are some of the judgments and expectations I've heard partners express in relationships that not only survived but improved as a result of growing lighter about each other's imperfections.

- "He's too aggressive."
- "He's too passive."
- "She's too outgoing."
- "She's too shy."
- "He's always talking about himself."
- "I wish he'd open up and tell me about himself."

- "She worries too much about money."
- "She doesn't consider where the money will come from."
- "He only thinks about his career."
- "I wish he'd give more thought to his career."
- "She's so opinionated."
- "She's so wishy-washy."
- "He's too sensitive."
- "I wish he were more sensitive."

When I showed the list to Marcie, she chuckled. "That's me," she said. "I used to enjoy just being with Victor, but ever since we started talking about our future, all I can see are his liabilities and shortcomings."

> ✗ *Part of becoming less judgmental is accepting that we all make judgments; the less you resist the fact that no partner will ever fit all your pictures, the more you can appreciate whomever you are with.*

Marcie's indecision about whether to live with Victor was clouded by far more than his quirks. Marcie had grown up with a great deal of care and affection until she was ten, when her parents went through a very difficult and painful divorce. As Marcie recalled, "My father used to be very interested in me and my schoolwork, but starting with their separation everything changed. Mom used to call him a loser, and they had terrible money fights. I would always take his side and defend him, but after the divorce when he didn't come to see us for several months, I had no choice but to side with her. He eventually did start calling and seeing us on weekends, yet it was never the same again."

Marcie's feelings of betrayal made her extra-sensitive to being disappointed by Victor. Her fear of getting hurt again became all too clear when she and Victor began negotiating over a condominium. According to Marcie, "I went nuts when Victor proposed that we write in a clause about how to divide our co-ownership in the event that we split up as a couple. 'Split up,' I shouted. 'I thought you were the one who was sure we ought to get married.'"

Quite often if we have been deeply disappointed or hurt by a parent, we may expect our adult partner to make up for everything we always wanted but never got. Marcie not only wanted Victor to love and be committed to her but she also secretly wanted him not even to consider leaving her, as her father had done when she was ten. As I explained to Marcie, just as she had doubts, fears, and worries about the chance of getting hurt again, so probably did Victor. She would need to sort out realistic expectations from those impossible demands for which Victor, or anyone else, could only let her down.

To help Marcie understand some of the demands and expectations she was bringing into this relationship, I asked her to write out a list of responses to the statement "If you truly loved me, Victor, you would——." Marcie's list included the following:

"If you truly loved me, you would..."

- Never want to leave me
- Have no second thoughts
- Never hurt or make me angry

- Be my dashing prince and always care for me
- Not look at another woman
- Work harder to be more successful
- Always be a dependable and loyal father
- Never lie to me
- Always find me sexy
- Do lots to make me happy
- Make sacrifices for your family

When Marcie and I went over her list, she recognized that some of her expectations were realistic while others were demands that neither Victor nor anyone else could possibly live up to. For example, expecting Victor to "have no second thoughts" or "never hurt or make me angry" was not likely to be possible. By recognizing some of the difficult demands she placed on a relationship, Marcie became more aware of unresolved hurts carried over from childhood. She saw that heavy demands are a self-fulfilling prophecy that eventually makes the other person go away. As Marcie eventually understood, "The reason I demand so much is because I'm so afraid that Victor or any man I love will disappoint and leave me."

> *Heavy demands are a self-ful-filling prophecy that eventually makes the other person go away.*

I explained to Marcie that she didn't have to make that fear magically go away. In fact, the more she recognized how this Achilles Heel—her fear of getting hurt again—worked, the less it would control her.

The key is becoming your own best parent instead of expecting your love partner to be the parent you never had. As you develop yourself, you will be less likely to expect the impossible or seek to control your love partner. The more you can fulfill yourself, the more you can lighten your demands into preferences. When you feel hurt and defensive, instead of turning against your love partner, use it as an opportunity to discuss what you both can do to make the relationship more enjoyable. But remember to resolve the issue, not talk it to death. If you pay attention only to the problems in your relationship, soon that's all you will have. Acknowledge one another for the strengths and joy in your relationship.

A few weeks later Marcie and Victor had worked out the details of buying a condominium together. During the first year they lived together, difficult issues came up, but Marcie found that by being honest about her fears and expectations she no longer needed to make ultimatums or crawl back into a protective shell. As Marcie described in a follow-up session one year later, "Victor and I are doing great. Now that I'm allowing him to be himself, he's become incredibly understanding and loving. We're getting married in the spring and plan to have a child soon. I'm still insecure sometimes, but it doesn't get in the way anymore."

> ✗ *As you develop yourself, you will be less likely to expect the impossible or seek to control your love partner. The more you can fulfill yourself, the more you can lighten your demands into preferences.*

Healing After a Marital Breakup

A divorce decree may settle property, alimony, and custody issues, but there still remain unresolved emotional conflicts following the breakup of a marriage. We pay a terrible price for having an incomplete and strained relationship with an ex-spouse, especially when there are children involved. No matter how we try to justify our resentments or believe we have the past "handled," we suffer emotional wounds and even ill health from any unfinished business of the heart.

In this case, the Achilles Syndrome works like this: You may feel that keeping up your defenses is the only way to relate to your ex or that "what's done is done." You fear resolving the problem, lest it be too painful. You function as a competent adult in other areas of life, and yet in dealing with your ex you still sometimes feel like a helpless and victimized child. Underneath your protective exterior you may harbor painful, conflicting feelings. You may still feel some love while at the same time you can't stand your ex. You avoid sharing your true feelings for fear your hidden resentments will explode. You try not to show any vulnerability for fear of reopening old wounds. It feels too risky to be angry and too painful to be loving.

> *No matter how we try to justify our resentments or believe we have the past "handled," we suffer emotional wounds and even ill health from any unfinished business of the heart.*

If you fear getting hurt again, a difficult former marriage can undermine your ability to develop trust and happiness with your current love partner. To assess whether you still have unresolved feelings from your previous relationship, consider the following:

- Do you recognize when a situation in your current love life has been triggered by some unresolved issue in your former relationship?

- Are you troubled by fears of rejection, abandonment, or being trapped based on a previous bad experience?

- Do you and your ex require your children, family, and friends to choose sides?

- Do you engage in overeating or alcohol abuse as if to say, "See what you did to me? It's your fault"?

- Have you come to terms with any feelings of guilt or regret about your divorce?

- Are you able to express anger with your ex without turning it inward or reacting with blind rage?

- Is your current fulfillment still inhibited by bitter memories from your previous relationship?

- Do you feel restricted in expressing love for a new partner?

- Do you find yourself hiding your own strengths or becoming overly meek, "nice," and compliant to please a new partner?

- Have you learned all you can from your previous marriage about how to build a lasting love relationship?

Why bother, or who cares, you might say? It is not primarily for your ex, but for *you*. Fulfillment in your current love relationship depends on successfully healing and learning from past hurts. Unless you are willing to do so, your Achilles Heel will persist and similar conflicts may appear in the future. Nothing can take away the pain and disappointment of a failed marriage, yet learning from it is essential to moving forward. After you deal with your old relationship, you will be strong enough to risk yourself in a new one.

> *Fulfillment in your current love relationship depends on successfully healing and learning from past hurts. Unless you are willing to do so, similar conflicts may appear in the future.*

Gloria's case illustrates the value of learning and growing from a difficult marriage. A high school teacher who lives alone, Gloria entered therapy to work on her difficulties with men, including her ex-husband, Roger. As she described it when she first came to my office, "The struggles I face with five overcrowded classes of high school students are a piece of cake compared with the aggravation from my ex-husband."

Even though Gloria and Roger have been divorced for almost a year and have no children, their lives remain emotionally intertwined. According to Gloria, "We seem to be competing for the loyalties of old friends. Two couples we used to socialize with keep getting caught in the middle of our jealous and spiteful games. I ask them how Roger's doing and he asks how I'm doing. Our friends feel like they're spies and resent it."

Gloria felt her unresolved anger toward Roger was causing her to be defensive with other men. She admitted, "Every time I meet a new man, I find myself checking him out with a fine-tooth comb. Any similarities to Roger and I pull back. The trouble is that sooner or later they all do something that reminds me of the awful times in my first marriage."

Even though Gloria wanted to be open-minded about the possibilities of finding someone to love, her Achilles Heel of not wanting to get hurt again was undermining her judgment and holding back her finest qualities. As she described it, "I'm so afraid of letting myself get too emotionally involved with anyone. What guarantee do I have that it will turn out any better the next time?"

To help Gloria let go of her residual doubts and fears, I suggested an exercise that has helped many men and women complete their relationship with an ex and get on with their lives. Using guided imagery, you visualize your ex accepting your hurt and resentment as well as understanding fully your point of view. Regardless of how your ex would *actually* respond to your resentments and regrets, in this exercise imagine him or her giving you all the love, support, and respect that you deserve.

> **NOTE: Anyone with a history of psychiatric disorder or who feels emotionally unstable should not do this exercise without first consulting a qualified mental health professional.**

This exercise is designed to heal the lingering hurts from your marital breakup. *Under no circumstances should you use the regrets and resentments from this exercise to hurt or attack your ex-spouse.* You are healing old wounds from your former marriage in order to get on with your life. *You do not need to share these painful feelings with your actual ex-spouse in order to benefit from this exercise.* The healing takes place primarily within yourself and need not involve your ex-spouse directly.

Find a comfortable spot where you can be undisturbed for thirty minutes. Unplug the phone and put a Do Not Disturb sign on the door. Close your eyes, relax, and visualize you and your ex in an appropriate setting, perhaps your current home or the home you shared. If you find it difficult to visualize your ex, express your feelings while looking at an old photograph of him or her.

With your ex-spouse's image in mind, say in your own words, "Out of the respect I have for you deep down and out of the respect that underneath it all you have for me, there are some things I need to clean up with you." Now proceed to let your ex know the resentments and regrets you still harbor. Each painful memory or hurt should be described as specifically as possible. Detail is important. It is not helpful to use generalizations like "I never loved you" or "I wish I'd never met you." Instead, remember an incident, feeling, or conflict that upset you and describe your feelings to the visualized image of your ex-spouse.

It is not important to cover every hurt of your entire relationship. You may want to spend an entire session or two on a major traumatic event. Imagine you have complete permission from your ex finally to "let it out." As you describe your resentments and regrets, give yourself permission to release any anger, rage, or sadness. Play-act, exaggerate your feelings, scream—do anything to let your feelings go. Pound a pillow or mattress nearby to help you release these feelings physically. If you are afraid of making too much noise, shout into a pillow or turn your stereo up loud. You are *not* to wallow in your hurts but to release them safely. If you become distracted or feel emotionally blocked, don't strain but gently bring yourself back to the process. Remember that your intention is not to harm your actual ex-spouse. Rather, you are using this imagery to heal your old hurts safely and to move on.

After doing this exercise for approximately twenty minutes, you may feel satisfied or else emotionally fatigued. Lie down, take a few deep breaths, and let yourself unwind. Sometimes the exercise will feel more powerful than at other times. Every session will be different. If your marriage breakup was extremely painful, the release may take more than a few sessions. You should repeat the exercise once or twice a week for several weeks until you feel your "heavy" resentments and regrets lose their intensity and become significantly lighter.

Before you end the exercise, there is one more crucial step. Take a few deep breaths and imagine a healing light sweeping over both you and your ex. The light can be seen as emanating from any source comfortable to you—God, universal spirit, or love. Just as warmth and light can assist the healing of a physical wound, so this inner light can assist you in healing the pain and bitterness of your marital breakup. You have released the venom from your emotional abscesses; now is the time to let yourself heal. Relax deeply for five or ten minutes to complete your "treatment."

Do not resume your normal activity until you feel at ease and have completed the exercise. If you have a lingering pressure in your head or some irritability, take additional time to rest and unwind. Be careful not to take out any lingering feelings from this exercise on friends or loved ones.

Gloria found using this healing visualization extremely powerful. As she described it, "I pictured Roger and me sitting in my den, and all sorts of feelings came up. Anger for the things he'd done. Some guilt for the things I'd done. A lot of sadness that we'd had such high hopes and then messed it up completely." Among her resentments and regrets were the following:

- "I resent the way you promised to get along with my father but then never really tried."

- "I resent that I had to be the one to apologize after we had a fight."

- "I resent the times I made love when I didn't want to."

- "I regret the way I let you insult and yell at me because you were in a lousy mood."

- "I regret that I let you make the decisions on our major financial investments."

- "I regret not going for my master's degree because you felt threatened."

Enlightenment is about lightening up, allowing your emotional "heavies" to become lighter. Gloria related, "For the first time I could fully express myself. I didn't have to defend myself against his angry tirades. After ten minutes of doing the exercise, tears came streaming down my face. I felt so relieved to get this bitterness out of my system."

Following several sessions, Gloria noticed, "I'm a lot

more relaxed and genuine now in the way I relate to other men. The panic of searching for Mr. Right and fearing I'll make a mistake is gone. Instead of feeling terrified and putting each man I see through unfair tests, I can enjoy myself and be more loving."

Mending a Broken Heart

Late one Sunday afternoon Louis was doing some work he'd brought home from the office while his two sons were playing in the backyard. He had expected his wife to be home from shopping by now, since they had plans to attend a cousin's birthday party. Then the phone rang. The unfamiliar voice of a highway patrol officer informed him that his wife, Suzanne, had been in a head-on car accident and moments ago had died on the way to the hospital. Louis froze. How could this be happening? Was it some sort of awful joke? For several minutes he sat stunned and then called the boys in to tell them what had happened to their mother. Together, the three went to the hospital and began the painful process of making arrangements for the funeral.

That was two years ago. Sitting in my office, Louis looks as though it could have been yesterday. There are dark circles under his eyes. His expression still reflects shock and disbelief. When he speaks about his ex-wife and their relationship, he becomes visibly more animated, but soon finds himself struggling against tears.

"There is no one like her," he says of Suzanne, "so strong, warm, creative, loving. She always knew what I was thinking and what I needed. The boys idolized her. They're lost without her. It just hasn't been the same. It was as close to a perfect marriage as I could ever want. No one can ever replace Suzanne." The tears begin to flow.

Soon they become deep, wrenching sobs.

No loss is more painful or difficult to overcome than the loss of someone you love. The death of a spouse may be one of the most painful emotional experiences a human being can endure.

Following the death of a spouse there is a normal period of emotional turmoil that often persists for up to a year. Depression, reduced interest in other people, crying spells, and reduced vitality are natural parts of the healing process during recovery from such a loss. Normally, the process goes through stages: shock and denial, anger and depression, followed eventually by acceptance and letting go.

> ✗ *The death of a spouse may be one of the most painful emotional experiences a human being can endure.*

For Louis the healing process has gotten stuck. Two years later, depression still dominates. He is filled with bitterness that his wife died and left him. He has turned his anger inward and feels guilty for not doing more for her when she still lived. He thinks of her constantly and has no interest in other women. Unwilling to let go of mourning, Louis thinks his misery is a way of honoring her. He has little energy or enthusiasm for his work. Sleep is a problem, and he often cries for no apparent reason. He feels inadequate raising his two sons alone.

The Achilles Syndrome gave Louis a false protection from his pain and kept him from recovering. If these symptoms are allowed to persist over years, there is a real risk that the loss will never heal and that the person will remain chronically depressed. Louis was fortunate enough to have a close friend who insisted that he seek help.

When Louis described his wife and their relationship, the reason he was unable to recover from her death gradually became clear. Looking back, he could see their marriage only in terms of ideals: They had a perfect marriage. Suzanne was a woman without equal. She could do no wrong, and he could never be happy without her.

Of course, no one and no marriage is ever perfect. Louis's inability to recall Suzanne or their marriage in anything less than ideal terms was a tip-off. Behind Louis's idealized memories was a torrent of anger he couldn't accept. The idealized memories kept the unacceptable anger at bay, but at the cost of unresolved grief and depression.

Anger is a normal response to loss. When you lose someone you love, it is completely natural and healthy to feel angry at him or her for leaving you. It doesn't matter whether the person walked out on his or her own or was the victim of a tragic accident. The reason for the loss makes little difference to the underlying emotional chemistry. Loss results in hurt, which triggers anger. This is a law of the functioning of the human psyche. To heal from the loss of a love, anger must be accepted and ventilated so that the pain of the hurt can be fully let go. When the anger is denied, the price is incomplete healing and chronic depression.

> *To heal from the loss of a love, anger must be accepted and ventilated so that the pain of the hurt can be fully let go. When the anger is denied, the price is incomplete healing and chronic depression.*

Like most people, Louis could not admit his anger toward his deceased spouse because his anger made him feel guilty. He loved her; she was such a good friend and partner. She was taken away by a freak accident. How could he dare feel, much less express, anger toward her? That was Louis's reasoning. He failed to recognize that anger following a loss, especially of someone you love deeply, isn't rational. It simply is. It must be resolved if healing is to complete its full cycle.

Louis owed it to himself and his two sons to complete his mourning fully. The most honest way to respect the memory of a loved one is to accept and understand the loss. While there may never be anyone quite like the person who died, there will be another person whom you can love and feel loved by.

> ✗ *The most honest way to respect the memory of a loved one is to accept and understand the loss. While there may never be anyone quite like the person who died, there will be another person whom you can love and feel loved by.*

When Louis understood that it was okay to recover from this most painful of human experiences, he was able gradually to stop punishing himself. He agreed that Suzanne would not have wanted him to wallow in misery and would have wanted him to create a new life for himself and the children. Gradually he grew able to talk about Suzanne as she was, not as the ideal he had created. Finally, he was willing to risk exploring all his feelings about Suzanne's death.

Difficult issues began to come up. How did he feel about being left alone with two children? What about his sexual needs? What about his need for a companion and friend? Did he fear that if he got involved with someone else, it was going to dishonor Suzanne? Did he fear that if he let down his defenses, he might get hurt again? Perhaps Suzanne wasn't simply the ideal person he remembered. Perhaps she, like anyone else, had some faults. Perhaps he was angry with her for leaving him.

A simple exercise broke the dam of his feelings and helped Louis let go of his regrets and *if only*'s. Following my instructions, Louis set aside an hour of complete privacy. Unplugging the phones and putting a Do Not Disturb sign on the door of his study, he sat down with a pen and pad of paper, a box of tissues, and a series of old photographs of Suzanne and himself.

Since most people find this to be an emotionally trying exercise, you should make sure to give yourself enough time and privacy to work through your feelings fully. For most, the exercise takes from thirty minutes to an hour. It should be repeated a few times at first and then whenever excessive guilt or depression has you shut down.

As though writing a letter to your departed spouse, list your most painful regrets. Include the things you would like to have told to or done with your spouse while he or she was still alive. For many, these memories and feelings come easily. For some, regrets are deeply submerged and will take more time to surface. That's why it's valuable to repeat this exercise at least a few times.

Louis found that looking at a photograph of Suzanne taken shortly before she died helped him get in touch with his long-suppressed rage and helplessness. As I had suggested, he didn't hold back his anger but acted it out safely by pounding a pillow. When you lose someone you love, you have a right to feel hurt and angry. The critical point for Louis was to accept the anger without feeling guilty.

Louis's list of regrets and *if only*'s follows:

- "I regret that you left me without our having a chance to say good-bye."

- "I regret you left me alone with two sons who really need you."

- "I regret that I didn't tell you enough how much I loved and respected you."

- "I regret that you and I always talked about the future and never got to share it."

- "I regret that I watched a football game every Sunday instead of spending more time with you."

- "If only we hadn't been so busy the last couple of weeks you were alive."

- "If only you'd been less hung up on cleaning the house, we'd have had more good times together."

- "If only we hadn't had that stupid quarrel about the party the day before you died."

- "If only it had been me that died and not you."

With the gradual release of his guilt and anger, Louis's depression began to lift. No longer did he hide behind the false "security blanket" of the fear of getting hurt. No longer did he need to hold on to an idealized memory of

Suzanne and their marriage. He could begin to appreciate the past as it was: wonderful in many ways but not perfect. Remaining distraught was no longer proof of how much he loved his wife. He could accept the tragedy for what it was. The greatest testimony to Suzanne was to pick up the pieces now for himself and his family. This is the stage of understanding that gives courage in the face of tragedy. Although Louis knew it would take time before he was ready to share his life with a new love partner, he now felt more ready to move forward. While his Achilles Heel would ache a bit, it would no longer cripple him or his sons.

"I Thought I Could Trust Him"

Almost every intimate relationship at some time deals with jealousy. Some couples pretend jealousy is only for those in less-perfect relationships—until the emergence of a "sudden" affair. Other couples go to the opposite extreme of watching each other like prison guards. Every conversation turns into an inquisition: "Where were you?" "What did he (she) look like?" "How do I know you're not lying?" or "How can I trust you when you do this to me?" Jealousy is sometimes the surest way to get rid of the very person you are afraid of losing.

An affair often produces a severe crisis of mistrust, rage, and betrayal. This is true whether the couple is married or has an "understanding." Once two people feel coupled, outside affairs are very hurtful. But in marriage it is worse. The public statement they've made to their family and community makes infidelity more painful. The stakes are also much higher when children, property, and shared history are jeopardized by an affair.

> ✗. *Jealousy is sometimes the surest way to get rid of the very person you are afraid of losing.*

Even if the affair happened years ago, the Achilles Heel of being afraid of getting hurt again can paralyze your relationship. It can make both partners so cautious or so cavalier that intimacy and trust are gone. In a marriage or long-term relationship jealousy can often reduce both partners to their most childish and possessive selves. One partner, forever worried about getting caught or having a past indiscretion discovered, views the other partner as the suspicious enemy. The other partner suffers the humiliation and uncertainty of never knowing for sure if a loved one is being honest or covering up.

Elizabeth's case illustrates the challenge of overcoming jealousy and rebuilding a marriage after a destructive affair. An attractive woman in her early forties, Elizabeth has been married to her husband, Michael, for twenty-four years. She came to my health center complaining of tension in her neck and lower back as well as difficulty sleeping. When Elizabeth talked about her relationship with Michael, her face became tense and her voice constricted: "The tension in my back started two years ago, around my fortieth birthday. I had been feeling a little sluggish and overweight. Rather than just complaining, I wanted to do something, so I asked Michael if I could splurge and spend two weeks at a health spa in Mexico. For my birthday I would come back fit and trim as a wonderful present to him.

> ✗ *In a marriage or long-term rela-*
> *tionship jealousy can often reduce both*
> *partners to their most childish and*
> *possessive selves.*

"He didn't want me to go. We'd never been apart more than a few days in all the years we'd been married, but finally he gave in. For two weeks I got up early every morning to jog, eat lightly, and exercise. When I got off the plane, I really looked good. I was expecting Michael to take me home and make passionate love to me.

"Michael seemed unusually quiet as we were driving home. Suddenly, he blurted out that while I was gone, he'd had an affair with Adrienne, his frequent tennis partner and someone I thought was my best friend. I was in shock. After all, I thought I could trust him and never expected that he and Adrienne could do something like this to hurt me."

That night, Elizabeth felt as if her husband of twenty-two years was a stranger. Michael kept apologizing and assuring Elizabeth that it had only been a one-time thing. Elizabeth recalls feeling numb, unable to get angry, and so hurt she wondered about whether or not to end the relationship.

The next morning, Elizabeth called another of her close friends, Caroline, for advice and consolation. Elizabeth remembers feeling her anger start to emerge as she described to Caroline what Michael and Adrienne had done. But rather than support Elizabeth in letting out her anger, this friend calmed her down and assured her that Michael still loved her and wouldn't make the same mistake again. Caroline argued, "As hard as this is for you, think of what he must be going through. It took real guts to be honest; most men would never have told."

Caroline urged Elizabeth to recognize how much she still loved Michael and didn't want to lose him. Taking Caroline's advice, Elizabeth made up her mind to view the affair the way Michael had described it—two lonely people who had made a terrible mistake and now were sorry. From that day until two years later, when she entered therapy, Elizabeth had convinced herself that she had forgiven Michael and that the affair was no longer the issue.

What you resist persists: Elizabeth pretended she was over the affair, yet there were many indications her conflicts were unresolved. Looking back, she could see that ever since the affair she had been afraid to spend a night away from Michael and felt anxious whenever he went out of town on business. She noticed herself judging her sexual performance more than usual and constantly looking for reassurance from Michael that she was still attractive. She was embarrassed, enraged, and uncomfortable whenever she ran into Adrienne at the tennis club.

No matter how hard she tried to be the loving and understanding wife, Elizabeth found herself questioning what had drawn Michael to Adrienne and worrying that he might look elsewhere again. She heard herself talking to Michael in a sarcastic tone and often made biting and hurtful remarks. Their emotional distance grew while their sex life diminished.

When we began working together, we discovered that underlying her physical symptoms was the Achilles Syndrome: Elizabeth's fear of being hurt that turned to bitterness and persistent physical symptoms. To help her work through the feelings she had tried to deny for almost two years, I suggested she write out her resentments toward Michael, Adrienne, and Caroline. The psychological importance of working through painful resentments cannot be underestimated. Not to release suppressed feelings of hurt and anger is to remain imprisoned by them.

> ✗. *The psychological importance of working through painful resentments cannot be underestimated. Not to release suppressed feelings of hurt and anger is to remain imprisoned by them.*

I urged Elizabeth to set aside time to write out her resentments and acknowledge whatever emotions came up. Once she started her list, tears and anger began to pour out. Here is a partial list of Elizabeth's resentments:

"I resent Michael for . . ."

- Using our home for his affair
- Expecting me to be understanding
- Asking me what I thought he should say to get rid of Adrienne
- Making it sound like he was the one suffering more
- Pretending the issue was gone even though I was seething
- Blaming our diminished sex life on me
- Staring at other women when we're at dinner parties
- Getting upset whenever I asked him for reassurance
- Acting so cool and self-assured

"I resent Adrienne for ..."

- Screwing Michael
- Telling me it was no big deal
- Humiliating me
- Looking so arrogant when I see her
- Sending Michael a birthday card at the office

"I resent Caroline for ..."

- Telling me to be strong when I needed to cry
- Convincing me that if I got angry, I would lose Michael
- Being all smiles and "Isn't everything wonderful" ever since

When Elizabeth wrote out her resentments, she felt a huge load lift from her shoulders. The purpose of this exercise is not to punish anyone or wallow in your pain, but to release bitter feelings safely. Give yourself comfort and encouragement as you recall the pain when a loved one betrayed you. Feel free to cry, pound a mattress, or scream into a pillow as you release these resentments from your system.

(Please note: These resentment lists are never meant as ammunition to hurt anyone. Your Achilles Heel is not caused by the person you're angry at, or by the painful incident. It is resolving *your* anger that will heal you. Then, when you let go of your bitterness and feel more at peace, you will be in a better position to initiate a constructive dialogue with whoever upsets you. By first completing your own psychological housecleaning, you will be better able to share both your anger *and* your love.)

Despite her stated resentments, Elizabeth loved Michael

and wanted their marriage to be wonderful again. After an affair many couples put a lid on their anger and never successfully work through their deep hurts. Others react with blind rage and walk out of even the most satisfying relationship when their partner commits an infidelity.

The challenge for Elizabeth was to break through their emotional distance and mistrust. To begin healing their marriage, I suggested she write a special love letter containing some of the feelings she had been reluctant to share. With most married couples, underneath the anger there is hurt; underneath the hurt there is love. While many people respond to an affair by issuing ultimatums, rules, and claustrophobic protections, a carefully written love letter can be healing.

> *With most married couples, underneath the anger there is hurt; underneath the hurt there is love.*

A Love Letter

The most effective love letter has the following three parts:

1. *The release of hurt and anger without dumping on your partner.* Rather than piling accusations on your partner, express your pain in a way that can be most appreciated. By using "I" statements, such as "I felt betrayed when . . . ," "I still feel unresolved about . . . ," or "I feel insecure about . . . ," you take responsibility for your feelings. If you avoid accusatory "you" statements, such as "You did this" or "You did that," your partner is likely to be less defensive and more receptive.

2. *The acknowledgment that you both can grow from the incident.* Don't be afraid to admit how you might have contributed to the marital tensions and miscommunication that led to the affair. The issue is not blame or fault but to learn what can be improved to rebuild love and trust in your relationship.

3. *The expression of love, trust, and intimacy.* You don't have to pretend you don't love your spouse to punish him or her. In fact, the more you can express your feelings of tenderness, the more easily your partner can acknowledge your pain. Forgiveness doesn't mean forgetting, nor does it mean whitewashing what has happened. Forgiveness means letting go, moving on, and favoring the positive.

> *Forgiveness doesn't mean forgetting, nor does it mean whitewashing what has happened. Forgiveness means letting go, moving on, and favoring the positive.*

Elizabeth gathered her courage and after several days of work on her letter wrote as follows:

Dear Michael,

Out of the love I have for you and the commitment to our marriage being all that it can be, there are some things I need to share. I bring up this unfinished business out of a sincere desire to complete it and be more loving.

I really did both of us a disservice by being so nice

and understanding right after you told me about the affair. I'm glad you told me, but inside I was burning up. Not just with anger for you, but also for Adrienne, who should have said no, and for Caroline, who told me to put on a smiling face and not risk sharing my anger with you. I have become much too insecure about myself and much too critical and snappy at you since the affair. I love you so much and have needed to share what's been going on inside me.

Part of me needed to say and never got the chance, "You stupid bastard. How could you do that, especially with my best friend?" I'm not the understanding angel I sometimes pretended to be. In fact, I really never bought the idea that you were so lonely you had to do it. You chose to, you stinker, and didn't consider my needs at all.

At the same time, I can see you're human and can make mistakes. I forgive you. I love you and our life together. I want us to understand each other even better and grow from this. When you or I are unhappy with something in our relationship, we need to talk. Let's make our marriage better than it ever was.

I love you,

Elizabeth

After Michael read the letter, they talked and wept together for several hours. According to Elizabeth, "This was a huge breakthrough for us because we had been walking on eggshells ever since the affair. Michael told me he felt relieved to talk about what we both knew had been hurting us. Michael still felt guilty and blamed himself for our emotional distance."

Elizabeth and Michael sought marital counseling to improve communication and begin moving forward. As I explained to them, in an intimate relationship we are constantly changing and evolving as individuals and as a couple. For love to remain vital we need constantly to rediscover our partner and not assume we already know him or her. Then the "I love you's" don't become insincere and automatic but take on a renewed meaning.

Elizabeth's backaches and insomnia gradually cleared up as she let go of her fear of being hurt. Feeling inspired, Michael and she decided to renew their wedding vows and go on a second honeymoon. At their recent silver wedding anniversary, Elizabeth confided in me that their sex and love life have reached a new level of intimacy.

3. Making Peace With Your Body & Appearance: "When I Look in the Mirror, I'm Never Quite Satisfied"

How do you feel about your body? Recall how you felt the last time you glanced in your bathroom mirror or when you walked past a store window or mirrored office divider. What "flaws" did you notice? When you stopped to look at your reflection, did you smile and say, "Hey, you look terrific!" or did you immediately focus on something that didn't seem quite right? We invest a tremendous amount of energy in how we look, and therein lies an extremely draining Achilles Heel. As Anaïs Nin noted, "Every one of us carries a deforming mirror where he sees himself too small or too large, too fat or too thin, even you who see yourself so free, blithe and unscarred. Once the deforming mirror is smashed, there is the possibility of wholeness, the possibility of joy."

You might say you aren't overly concerned with your looks, yet what happens when your love partner stares at someone who is especially attractive? How does it feel when you notice signs you are putting on weight or getting older? How confident are you being seen in your bathing suit or undressing in front of a romantic partner? When you look at photographs of yourself, do you criticize your appearance mercilessly, or do you avoid anyone taking your picture in the first place? How much time and money do you spend trying to make yourself look more youthful, slim, or attractive? Do you ever truly reach the point of being satisfied, or is your appearance a struggle that never gets easier?

When we think about it, we realize that our value as a person doesn't depend on how attractive we are. Yet try as we may to separate our self-worth from our looks, we continue to compare ourselves with others, especially with those in movies and advertising with flawless skin, beautiful figures, and classic features. In many instances we are still judging ourselves by criteria we learned in junior high school as to who was good-looking and popular versus who was gawky and unattractive. You probably have not forgotten what it felt like to be teased for your braces, glasses, clothes, blemishes, body type, or athletic clumsiness. Whereas we may outgrow the physical awkwardness of adolescence, the stigma of being called "metal mouth," "four eyes," "chubby," or "pizza face" never seems to disappear.

As the years pass, the fear of aging presents new dilemmas. Men begin to dread a receding hairline, bulging stomach, or unarousable penis; women seem especially threatened by wrinkles, cellulite, and gray hair. Instead of valuing our changing looks, we live with unrealistic either/or standards. We look either youthful or else "old." We are either painfully thin or else overweight. We are either musclebound and athletic or else terribly out of shape. Either we wear the latest fashion in clothes and hairstyle or else we are drab and old-fashioned.

Why, in order to identify some people as beautiful, do we need to define the rest of us as not so? Nearly every decade the rules seem to change. One decade large bosoms are in, and the next small bosoms are fashionable. One year short hair is attractive, and the next year thick permanent waves are a must. The yardstick by which we measure our looks is always too narrow to account for all the differences that make us unique.

Quite often the problem is compounded by traumatic past experiences. If your father turned cold or critical when your breasts began to develop, you may still feel uncomfortable about your sexual characteristics. If your parents belittled or teased you for the "unladylike" way you walked, dressed, or wore your hair, you may still feel wary about dressing casually. If as a boy you were called "sissy," you may fear ever appearing flamboyant or colorful. If a romantic partner was critical of your weight or appearance, you may still worry that your current lover will feel the same way. If you were ridiculed by a hairdresser or clothing salesperson, you may feel insecure when you go for a haircut or new clothes.

> *The yardstick by which we measure our looks is always too narrow to account for all the differences that make us unique.*

Even the most beautiful individuals can be insecure about their looks. One of my clients, among the most highly paid and most recognizable male models in the world, was terribly fearful about how others viewed him. Remarkably, he felt unattractive and nervous about dating because he had an almost imperceptible facial scar. Despite all the admiring stares he received, he was self-conscious, sure that people would judge him negatively because of his scar.

Like many whose self-worth depends on their looks, this model suffered from what I refer to as "pretty person's disease," the fear that the slightest flaw or change in appearance will cause others to be disappointed. When he looked in the mirror, he couldn't help noticing this tiny "flaw," and no matter how he tried, he couldn't dismiss his fears of being badly judged. Regardless of how close we come to the socially accepted ideal of beauty, we can't feel good about ourselves as long as we remain preoccupied with those parts of our body we can't accept.

The Social Feedback Loop

The great irony about looks is that far more important than your physical features are the feelings you radiate about yourself. If you judge yourself harshly, you send out messages to others that say, "Don't notice me," or "Without makeup I'd be a mess." Such self-criticism encourages others to underrate your attractiveness.

We focus most obsessively on the physical "flaw" we are most terrified of exposing. When a balding man attempts to cover up a bald spot by draping a long strand of hair over it, he communicates just how uncomfortable he is about losing his hair and focuses more attention on his bald spot. When a slightly overweight woman wears a black tent dress and complains constantly about her diet, how can anyone help but see her as fat? Yet by perceiving ourselves as somehow deficient and less worthy because of our physical "flaws," we make it hard for others to break through our discomfort and remind us of how truly attractive we may be.

The social feedback loop can also be used to feel good and positive about ourselves: What you put attention on in life grows stronger. If you signal that you are an energetic and attractive person, people will tend to see you that way. When your posture, eye contact, clothes, facial expressions, and attitude reflect self-confidence and self-acceptance, others are likely to trust and feel good about you as well.

Instead of projecting shame, embarrassment, or inhibition, you can communicate that you are beautiful regardless of whether you fit this year's cover girl or macho image. As Eleanor Roosevelt discovered, "No one can make you feel inferior without your consent." If you can develop a more loving attitude toward yourself, you will convey to others how attractive you are.

We have all known a few unusually tall, short, or heavy people who are so relaxed and self-assured that we found them extremely attractive without a second thought about how they compared with the social norm. There are men whose baldness does not detract one iota from their handsomeness, individuals whose Roman nose is a stunning asset rather than a source of shame or discomfort. Beauty may be in the eyes of the beholder, but the person who determines how others will judge your appearance is you.

Feeling dissatisfied and complaining about your looks is a habit that society, advertisers, and even our friends often reinforce. It is also a habit that may continue long after you have lost weight or improved your appearance. Many times the feeling of inadequacy is so familiar that, ironically, one feels uncomfortable living without it. The key to breaking this pattern is to examine and improve your own attitude toward your looks.

"Mirror, Mirror on the Wall..."

We each deserve to feel beautiful. More than just looking good on the outside, feeling beautiful means experiencing yourself as being attractive, sexy, and vibrant. Nothing is more appealing than genuine enthusiasm, and nothing inhibits enthusiasm more than self-criticism. Contrary to common belief, feeling beautiful does not lead to narcissism. It is the *lack* of good feelings about yourself that leads to self-absorption. The reason many people become obsessed with their appearance is not that they feel beautiful but that no matter how much they strive to improve their looks, they still consider themselves unattractive. Truly feeling good about yourself—inside and out—allows you to move beyond self-absorption to the ability to give more genuinely of yourself.

Learning fully to accept and appreciate how you look isn't easy. Everyone seems to have something to change. What is your complaint? Is it your hips, belly, butt, thighs, nose, complexion, teeth, hairline, or posture? Most of us deprecate ourselves for one or more physical characteristics. Instead of saying, "This is me and this is how I look," we spend excess time and money attempting to look like some media image.

> *Feeling beautiful does not lead to narcissism. It is the* lack *of good feelings about yourself that leads to self-absorption.*

In order to stop feeling dissatisfied when you look in the mirror, you must first become more aware of what you do. To recognize the judgments you make about your looks, stand naked in front of a full-length mirror. Look at yourself front, back, and side. Write down or make a tape recording of the thoughts, feelings, and judgments that come to mind. Most people find there is a lot they don't like. Some examples of common responses are the following:

- "Potbelly"
- "Messy hair"
- "Dry skin"
- "Penis too small"
- "Flabby thighs"
- "Breasts sag"
- "Breasts too small"
- "Bad posture"
- "Skin blemishes"
- "Not enough muscle"
- "Cellulite"
- "Love handles"

As you began to notice just how much you criticize your looks, continue to look at yourself and see what other thoughts and feelings come to mind. It is normal to experience a variety of emotions while doing this exercise. Standing naked in front of the mirror may bring up feelings of embarrassment, anger, rage, frustration, arousal, happiness, and even tremendous joy. Let any feelings arise; don't be afraid to cry. These painful judgments from childhood and adolescence have been stuffed inside you while you did your best to pretend nothing bothered you. Now is the time to give up pretending and to acknowledge your self-criticisms and let them go. Remember that your purpose in listing your judgments about your body is not to punish yourself but to love yourself fully.

While you're looking self-critically into the mirror, notice whether your chest seems tight and your breathing constricted. Do you appear anxious or insecure? Feeling dissatisfied when you look in the mirror is a self-fulfilling prophecy. Your shoulders slump and your stomach protrudes as if you are being weighed down with a heavy burden. Your eyes lose their sparkle, and the lines on your face grow deeper. It's difficult for anyone to smile or act enthusiastic when feeling self-reproach and disapproval. Chronic self-criticism makes us look and feel much older than our years.

Now imagine several balloons lifting up your shoulders and straightening your spine so that your stomach pulls in and your pelvis tilts forward. Breathe deeply and smile. Now look at yourself. Notice how much stronger and more vibrant you look when your chest is full and your head held high. You needn't take on the rigid look of a military recruit. Relax your shoulders, breathe deeply in and out, and see if you don't feel more satisfied with your looks.

How comfortable are you when your appearance reflects more confidence and power? For many of us, standing up straight and exuding strength may feel awkward, different, or "not me." To appreciate your looks fully may require breaking a habit of self-image you have had for many years. One of the definitions of the word *habit* is "costume" or "suit of clothes." In fact, you have been wearing the habit of dissatisfaction with your looks for too long. You are going to try on a new habit, to practice seeing yourself in a different light.

Your Most Important Beauty Exercise

Whenever you look in the mirror, you make a basic choice to feel either satisfied or dissatisfied. Feeling dissatisfied may be so ingrained and automatic that it is difficult to change. Yet thousands of men and women I have worked with have successfully broken the vicious cycle of self-criticism through using a simple, powerful technique. Rather than looking in the mirror and feeling dissatisfied, give yourself the following "beauty treatment":

1. Set aside twenty minutes and make sure you will not be disturbed.

2. Take the phone off the hook and stand nude or seminude in front of a full-length mirror.

3. Breathe deeply, stand erect with your shoulders back, and now with conviction declare, "I am beautiful." Allow whatever resistances you have to come up and then repeat.

4. Look at each part of your body and tell yourself with enthusiasm, "I am beautiful." Notice how different it feels to be affirming your looks rather than finding fault. If negative comments and judgments come to mind, just notice them and go back to affirming, "I am beautiful."

5. Give repeated doses of "I am beautiful" to the parts of your body of which you have been the most critical.

6. To complete the exercise, give yourself a kiss on the back of the hand as you look in the mirror and say, "I am beautiful." Don't be embarrassed. It's no crime to feel good about yourself; to the contrary, it's harmful not to. Remember that feeling beautiful allows you to stop obsessing over your looks and to start putting your energy into more important activities.

Clients who have done this exercise report remarkable breakthroughs in their ability to accept their bodies and feel more attractive. I have done this exercise in bathing suits with severely physically handicapped and deformed men and women, both individually and in a group. With severe burn victims or those with missing limbs, extra care was taken to handle the deep emotional obstacles to self-acceptance. Yet I have found repeatedly there is no physical barrier to experiencing yourself as beautiful, only your belief.

> *There is no physical barrier to experiencing yourself as beautiful, only your belief.*

This "beauty treatment" can be informative and rewarding only if you overcome your own resistance. I've listed here several typical lines clients have used to keep from appreciating themselves. Note that in each case the statement "I am beautiful" is followed by the immediate response that came to that person.

Experience	Response
"I am beautiful."	"If I'm beautiful, what's ugly?"
"I am beautiful."	"It sounds so conceited."
"I am beautiful."	"I hope my husband doesn't catch me doing this."
"I am beautiful."	"I'm cute. I *wish* I were beautiful."
"I am beautiful."	"I used to be until I let myself go."
"I am beautiful."	"Maybe if I lost ten pounds."
"I am beautiful."	"Are you kidding?"
"I am beautiful."	"Uggh."
"I am beautiful."	"Why is this so difficult?"
"I am beautiful."	"If only my hips were less puffy."
"I am beautiful."	"I wish I could say it and mean it."

A remarkable thing happens when you stand in front of the mirror long enough. As you continue to say, "I am beautiful," and release the judgments that come to mind, you will begin to notice features you like about yourself. You will become less self-conscious and more accepting. The trick is to hang in there beyond the initial stages of embarrassment and self-criticism. *Most people cheat themselves by quitting after their initial negative responses. Others cheat themselves by pretending they're satisfied and denying their judgments. Do this exercise for at least ten minutes to see what you look like once self-criticism no longer blocks your vision.* After you use this beauty treatment for ten days, feeling beautiful will no longer seem strange or impossible.

To assist my clients further, I ask them to find ten specific things they love about their looks. The instruction is to write down the words "I am beautiful" on the left and ten things you appreciate on the right.

Here is an illustration:

Experience	*Response*
"I am beautiful."	"I love my eyes."
"I am beautiful."	"My face reveals my warmth and wisdom."
"I am beautiful."	"I like the big comfortable look my body has."
"I am beautiful."	"My breasts have fed both my children."
"I am beautiful."	"I've earned those stretch marks and wear them with pride."
"I am beautiful."	"When I stand erect, I have a lot of strength in my upper torso."
"I am beautiful."	"I'm proud of my curvaceous figure."
"I am beautiful."	"My body has served me well."
"I am beautiful."	"I *am* beautiful, and it feels terrific."

In addition to these beauty treatments, you must commit yourself to no longer complaining about your looks. Complaining is just another way of putting yourself down. It took you decades to learn your insecurities, so you won't unlearn them overnight. Yet once you experience feeling genuinely good about your looks, you will feel you have come home. It will never be as easy or automatic to put yourself down. This Achilles Heel will rarely trouble you.

Your beauty treatment can be done either when you start your day or at night before going to bed. In addition, put an "I am beautiful" notecard on your bathroom mirror, refrigerator door, and the dashboard of your car. Find (or have someone take) a photograph of you that really shows your best feature. Carry that photo around with you to remind yourself that you *are* beautiful. An extra beauty treatment in front of a mirror can be helpful before an important date, job interview, or meeting. If you walk into those encounters feeling self-confident and beautiful, you will be amazed at the positive responses you receive.

The "I Am Beautiful" exercise makes it much easier to stick to a diet and exercise program. When you are sitting down to a good meal, jogging, doing aerobics, lifting weights, or getting a massage, say the words "I am beautiful" as you inhale and then breathe out negativity. When you put on swimwear or exercise clothes, new jeans or great new dress clothes, be sure to remind yourself that you are beautiful. When you undress in front of a lover, thinking "I am beautiful" enhances the way you look and feel.

Regularly using the "I Am Beautiful" exercise will result in others also looking more beautiful to you. The less harshly we judge ourselves, the more accepting we become of others. People want to be around you if you feel enthusiastic about yourself and others. Just as dissatisfaction with yourself is contagious, so is enthusiasm.

> ✐ *The less harshly we judge ourselves, the more accepting we become of others. Just as dissatisfaction with yourself is contagious, so is enthusiasm.*

The Fear of Fat

Gail's case is a good example of how powerful the "I Am Beautiful" exercise can be. A thirty-five-year-old client who had never been married, Gail came in hating herself for being ten pounds overweight. She had tried every diet, losing weight for a time, then gaining it back. An unhealthy pattern of periodically starving herself and then binging had been going on since early adolescence. According to Gail, "My parents always judged me by my looks. If I was thin, my mother showered me with compliments and my father showed me off to his friends. If I was overweight, they assumed I was being rebellious. My mother would warn, 'The way you look you'll never get married.'"

Severe anxiety over a relatively mild weight problem has become a common Achilles Heel. Obsession with being thin plagues not only those who are significantly overweight but also millions of under- and normal-weight people. Fad diets, appetite suppressants, and extreme self-consciousness about weight have become the rule of the day.

Gail's self-image was significantly hampered by her fear of being fat. Sitting in my waiting room in a slumped posture, wearing loose-fitting clothes, she seemed ten years older than she was. Her sad eyes seemed to communicate, "Don't notice me; I know I'm unattractive."

Like many people who judge themselves negatively because of their weight, Gail had tremendous difficulty accepting compliments or trusting that anyone could find her attractive. When her current boyfriend, Jason, would tell Gail that he liked the way she looked, she thought he was "just being polite" and seriously questioned his judgment. Like the Groucho Marx comment "I would never join a club that would have me as a member," an obsession with being thin makes it impossible to trust anyone who likes the way you look.

> ✗ *Like the Groucho Marx comment "I would never join a club that would have me as a member," an obsession with being thin makes it impossible to trust anyone who likes the way you look.*

When I suggested the "Mirror, Mirror" and "I Am Beautiful" exercises to Gail, she laughed out loud. "Are you kidding?" she said. "I'm smart, witty, and nice, but beautiful I'm not." Only with encouragement was she willing to try these exercises. Her initial responses to standing in front of a mirror in a bikini echoed criticisms she had heard from her parents:

- "I have no self-discipline."
- "I won't look good in this year's fashions."
- "I'm staying fat to avoid getting involved."
- "I'll never be thin."

- "I'm just lazy."
- "I have such a beautiful face . . . too bad it's wasted."
- "How can I go out looking like this?"

Like most people who have spent decades dieting and worrying about their weight, Gail was tired of fighting herself. Often the issue is not a lack of self-control, but a failure to combine self-control with self-acceptance. Unless you stop resisting your body type and heredity, your goals may be unrealistic. For example, Gail couldn't change the fact that she came from a long line of healthy, large-boned women who weren't built like today's fashion models. Her mother had big hips and thighs; her grandmother had them too. Only in Gail's generation did it suddenly become a "crime" to have a voluptuous build.

As I described to Gail, the cure for feeling fat is not necessarily just to get thin. As long as you resist seeing yourself as beautiful and lovable right now, the fear of being fat will continue to run you. Gail was surprised to learn that hating herself was an important reason why her weight problem persisted. Even when you diet and exercise, the important factor is the emotional atmosphere in which you do it. The key to effective and lasting weight control is not forcing yourself to eat what you "should" and exercising because you "have to." If you are constantly straining and beating yourself up, is it any wonder you feel like quitting your exercise program or stuffing your face the first chance you get? You may be caught in a Catch-22 where you don't want to attend an exercise class until you look great in leotards and you won't look good in leotards until you feel good about yourself right now! The only way to stick to a healthful program of nutrition and exercise is to learn to become a firm but always supportive coach.

After ten days of doing the "I Am Beautiful" exercise,

Gail's attitude began to change. As she describes it, "For the first time I started enjoying looking at myself in the mirror. I no longer felt embarrassed with my clothes off. After all, this is my body! I always used to cover my 'fat' belly with my hands. It was a reflex. Yesterday I caught myself doing it and put my hands behind my head like a model. I laughed with the pleasure of showing off. I'm a good-looking woman."

To maintain her positive attitude, Gail continued doing the "I Am Beautiful" exercise whenever she put on makeup, fixed her hair, or checked her appearance. Like many women, Gail usually gained a few pounds right before she got her menstrual period. By reminding herself that she was beautiful even when her weight fluctuated, she found it easier to stick to her diet and exercise regime. Putting on a few pounds is no reason to stop being your own number-one supporter and coach.

At her one-year follow-up appointment, Gail had lost fifteen pounds and looked terrific. She now dressed with more style and flair. More importantly, she had become more comfortable with her body. When her boyfriend told her she looked great, she could take the compliment to heart. Instead of her previous "You don't really mean it," she could feel good inside and respond with a simple "Thank You."

"Stop Picking on Yourself"

Another example of how "what you resist persists" can influence one's appearance is demonstrated by Bruce, a twenty-four-year-old graduate student with chronic acne. Despite being treated with a special diet, cleansers, and antibiotics, Bruce's acne remained severe, and he was referred to me by his dermatologist. Whenever his skin broke out,

Bruce would feel sorry for himself and say "Why me?" Anxiety about his blemishes hampered him in job interviews and on dates. Bruce blamed many of his difficulties on this Achilles Heel. He felt that as long as his skin broke out, he could never be successful or happy.

Like many with severe acne, Bruce was obsessed with keeping his face clean. Every night he would critically examine each new blemish and carefully squeeze those pimples that had come to a head. During the day Bruce fought a constant battle not to scratch or pick at his face.

When I asked Bruce to replace his nightly squeezing ritual with a simple facial rinse and the "I Am Beautiful" exercise, he became cynical and angry. "You want me to accept my pimples? Don't bet on it. I hate them." I explained the Achilles Syndrome to Bruce: "What you resist persists; picking on yourself just worsens the acne. Until you accept your skin exactly the way it is, you can't begin to improve it."

After further discussion, Bruce was motivated to do the "I Am Beautiful" exercise. Over the next week, he found that his response to saying "I am beautiful" included the following:

- "I hate looking like an awkward teenager."
- "I must be too sensitive."
- "If I was having sex more often, my skin would clear."
- "Women are turned off by my blemishes."
- "If I weren't so driven, I wouldn't have pimples."
- "I look ugly and immature."

Doing the exercise brought up a host of emotions for Bruce. Tears, anger, and painful memories of being laughed at for his pimples made him realize just how much he had learned to hate himself for his acne. As I emphasized to Bruce, this exercise was a safe way to release the emotional pain about his skin. I told him, "There is a great deal more to you than the acne on your face. Instead of thinking you have a shameful abnormality, you need to accept that you're attractive with or without clear skin. Like many people's, your skin flares up for various reasons: heredity, skin type, hormones, nutrition, stress, and polluted air. Beating yourself up and resisting the fact that your skin is sensitive only aggravates the problem. You're going to have to learn to love yourself exactly as you are, including your sensitive skin."

In addition to recommending that Bruce practice the "I Am Beautiful" exercise daily in front of the mirror, I suggested he look carefully at each blemish and say, "I accept that pimple. It's exactly where it should be and I am healing." After two weeks of doing this exercise, Bruce lost his compulsion to scratch and pick at his face. Over a period of months his skin became less inflamed and the pimples less noticeable. While Bruce's skin still flares up if he eats greasy foods or becomes too stressed, his acne now clears up in a day or two.

"I Dread Aging"

The billions of dollars spent annually to mask our age spots, gray hair, and wrinkles reflect our terrible fear of aging. We worry about a romantic partner leaving us for a younger mate. We fear being pushed aside in our careers by those who are our junior and less experienced. We find it more difficult to appreciate our beauty and vitality when signs of aging creep in.

Though aging happens gradually, sometimes its impact jolts us suddenly. You notice a college friend has a lot more gray hair since the last time you were together. During a holiday visit a parent seems to have become much older, and you wonder where the years have gone. You become sick or injured and worry about how that has left its mark on you. Your child reaches another milestone and you ask, "Have I changed that much, too?" You begin to think not only about how old you are but about how much time you have left.

The fear of growing older begins the first time we panic in front of the mirror and say, "Where did it all go?" Suddenly our faces seem to show the years of work and worry. What used to be a single gray hair has become widespread. The muscles that used to keep our breasts, belly, and rear end firm have now begun to droop. Our skin is drier and carved with the hard-earned wrinkles of experience. It's not as if people are saying out loud, "Oh my, you're growing older." Rather, it seems to show up in every mirror and is reflected in the eyes of the most important people we know.

Discomfort with growing older makes us question our sexual attractiveness. It's the reason we may be afraid to risk rejection. It may make us want to tell our sexual partner, "Don't notice my spare tire" or "Don't look at my bald spot." Yet once again, what you resist persists. Trying not to think about the signs of aging is like trying not to think of pink elephants. Thereafter, all you can think of is pink elephants.

Why can't we look at the physical signs of aging with as much pride as we have when we point to memorabilia, scrapbooks, and treasures? We can choose either to downgrade ourselves for sagging breasts and a spare tire or to see them as the trophies of a rich, full life. Rather than feeling embarrassed or apologizing for stretch marks, we can see them as the remnants of a job well done—losing weight or giving birth.

Accepting yourself doesn't mean ceasing to exercise or watch your diet. All growth is the integration of seemingly opposite values. As you get older, it means accepting yourself fully *and* taking responsibility for improving your physical and emotional fitness. When you live an active life, you tend to get fewer physical problems and you feel good about yourself.

> *Why can't we look at the physical signs of aging with as much pride as we have when we point to memorabilia, scrapbooks, and treasures?*

Whether you see your signs of aging as shameful flaws or as a natural process determines to a great extent how others will react to you. Although it cannot be denied that others will sometimes negatively judge you because of their own fear of aging, you hold tremendous power over how attractive you seem. Arlene's case illustrates how a person can seize that power and not downplay her looks or discount her value.

A forty-eight-year-old divorced woman with three grown children, Arlene came to therapy ostensibly to discuss her frustration at being alone after so many years as a wife and mother. Soon, however, Arlene revealed, "I dread aging. I'm young at heart, and yet all the men I meet treat me like I'm over the hill. Sometimes I feel like screaming, 'Hey, wait a minute. My time to live my own life has just begun.'"

Arlene had recently met her eldest daughter at a singles bar and was struck by the attention her daughter received. Arlene recalled how ashamed she felt "experiencing my own daughter as my competitor. It brought up all my insecurities about my looks and whether I'm still exciting to be with."

By underrating herself, Arlene was fueling a vicious cycle of rejection based on aging. Especially with society's excessive emphasis on youth, we need to be especially careful not to judge ourselves unfairly because we are getting older. To help Arlene see how her own judgments about aging were holding her back, I asked her to do the "Mirror, Mirror" and "I Am Beautiful" exercises. She immediately came up with several harsh judgments about herself, including the following:

- "No wonder my husband left me."
- "My best years are now gone."
- "No one wants to date a woman old enough to be a grandmother."
- "My hair looks ancient."
- "My skin makes me look older than my years."
- "Maybe I *am* over the hill."

I said to Arlene, "There are men who are so insecure about their looks or conditioned by superficial standards that they search for a woman half their age. But what about the men who know how to appreciate a woman with your background, intelligence, and good looks? You're attractive and energetic when you let yourself be. Yet you are probably communicating to men those same criticisms you give yourself in front of the mirror."

Turning What If's *Into* So What If's

Arlene then did an additional exercise to examine and over-come these insecurities further. To combat her fears of grow-ing older, Arlene learned to turn her *what if*'s into *so what if*'s. For example, Arlene had been raised to believe, "What if my hair turns gray? No one will find me attractive." Changing this *what if* into a *so what if* meant recognizing and accepting the fact that she could be truly beautiful with gray hair. Arlene did specific work on the following fears of aging:

What If's	*So What If's*
What if my breasts sag?	So what if my breasts sag. They're still sensuous.
What if someone sees my stretch marks?	So what if someone sees my stretch marks. I'm proud of having borne three children.
What if I have varicose veins?	So what if I have varicose veins. No one else is examining me with a microscope.
What if I have wrinkles?	So what if I have wrinkles. It's a souvenir of my wisdom.
What if someone thinks I'm too old?	So what if someone thinks I'm too old. It's their loss; I know I am beautiful.

As I reminded Arlene, the best way to find a mate is not in an impersonal singles bar but by participating in activities in which her energy could sparkle. With her self-confidence rising, Arlene interviewed for and got a job at her local public television station. Through her work she met several men who not only didn't have a problem with her age but found her very attractive and exciting. As Arlene describes, "The same woman who used to be 'over the hill' is now sexy and dynamic. When I look in the mirror these days, I see a beautiful and powerful human being."

4. Making Peace With Disapproval: "I Can't Stand Criticism"

Let's face it—none of us likes to be criticized, especially by those whose love and respect we want. Both giving and receiving criticism are difficult challenges that often lead to misunderstandings and hurt feelings. For example, during the past few weeks what specific incidents can you recall in which someone's criticism got under your skin? Did your spouse confront you with an old habit you were not ready to change? Did a parent say something that made you feel guilty or defensive? Did someone imply you weren't doing a good job?

What about their criticism made you feel angry or hurt? How did you respond? Did the situation get resolved or did you stuff your feelings inside?

Now recount a time in the past few weeks when someone got defensive because you were giving them criticism or advice. Is it easy for you to give criticism? Are you able to achieve a positive outcome or does it often lead to a conflict?

A very common Achilles Heel is our inability to give and receive criticism. We all struggle with it at one time or another. We're either accused of being "too sensitive" or else criticized for how we criticize! In this chapter you will learn more than how to tolerate criticism; you will learn to value it. That doesn't mean you have to comply with every piece of advice others give you, nor does it mean having to justify yourself or else rebel. Rather, you will learn to deal with criticism more effectively, without the usual struggles that plague love and work relationships.

> ✗ *We're either accused of being "too sensitive" or else criticized for how we criticize!*

Making Criticism Work for You

Criticism serves a vitally important function: We need feedback from others to learn what's working and what could be improved. If we discourage others from criticizing us, irritations and resentments pile up.

Just as criticism can cause problems, it can also help us understand what we want and need from one another. One of the greatest gifts you can give someone is to hear his or her anger, hurt, and criticism without becoming defensive. One of the greatest gifts you can receive is quality feedback about your opinions and behavior.

Making criticism work for you is essential to the success

of your business and personal relationships. For example, Carolyn is a highly talented interior designer whose livelihood and professional reputation depend on her ability to give and receive creative suggestions. Yet Carolyn admits, "I have as much trouble taking criticism as anyone else. When I design a plan, I get upset if my client or partners wrinkle their noses or disagree. Something in the way they say it or how I hear it leads me to take it personally."

> ✍ *One of the greatest gifts you can give someone is to hear his or her anger, hurt, and criticism without becoming defensive. One of the greatest gifts you can receive is quality feedback about your opinions and behavior.*

Especially if you're "the boss," a person with an administrative or executive position, it's extremely important not to shut yourself off from criticism. We all know the stories of people in high office whose mail, appointments, and even newspaper reading are censored to avoid presenting them with any criticism. When executives surround themselves with yes-men, employees are discouraged from offering needed suggestions or airing their grievances. Without criticism, minor problems go unsolved until they become major crises.

Quite often the more we care about someone, the harder it is to hear his or her criticism. Thomas is a personnel manager for a major corporation who prides himself on "how well I deal with people's feelings." Yet when his wife criticizes him at home, Thomas admits, "I don't take it very well. For instance, last Sunday morning my wife criticized the way I *always* get the floor soaking wet after I get out of the shower. I got defensive and started criticizing her for *always* leaving the cap off the toothpaste. This silly argument ruined brunch at our favorite restaurant."

How many times have you and your partner found yourselves stuck in a restaurant quarreling over some minor criticism? How often have you driven home in bitter silence with both of you feeling hurt? How much lost sleep or arguing over the phone did it take before you made up? Did you withdraw resentfully and bury the problem? Did an incident like this cause your relationship to end?

The paradox is that the more you resist criticism, the more of a problem it becomes; the more comfortable you become with it, the more you can make it work for you. Most of us did not learn in our families or education how to give and receive criticism effectively. In fact, our training was filled with bad examples where both the person dishing it out and the person receiving it felt angry, hurt, and dissatisfied.

Destructive Versus Constructive Criticism

There is value in distinguishing between two types of criticism and how they differ in intent, quality, and outcome. Destructive criticism is meant to put down, punish, or manipulate, and its effect is largely negative. Constructive criticism is supportive and empowering, with a commitment to a positive outcome.

Destructive criticism usually involves:

- A global, all-encompassing accusation that uses words such as *never*, *always*, *should*, and *ought* ("You *never* listen." "You *always* do this to me." "You *should* be more considerate." "You *ought* to know better.")

- An attempt to make the other person feel guilty ("You know how much I count on you." "I'm very disappointed in you." "This shows you don't really care.")

- An uncontrolled outburst of anger, impatience, or shouting to intimidate the other person ("Look at what you've done!" "This is the last straw!" "I hate you!")

- The use of old resentments as ammunition ("This is just like the time you . . ." "You remind me of my ex." "You're just like your mother.")

- The use of emotional blackmail, acting like a martyr ("It's really hard on me, but I feel it's my duty to point this out to you." "Telling you this hurts me more than it hurts you." "I'm wasting my breath talking to you.")

- Subtle and manipulative innuendoes to coerce the other person ("If you loved me, you'd . . ." "After all I've done for you, this is the thanks I get?" "Do what you want, but don't come crying to me.")

- A lengthy monologue in which one side dominates ("Let me finish. I've got more to get off my chest." "I don't want to hear your excuses." "You'll just have to wait.")

On the other hand, constructive criticism tends to be:

- Warm and supportive ("I liked your report, and we can talk about additional suggestions over lunch."

"Right now I'm not concerned with what happened but what we can do to make things right again.")

· Short and specific ("I like the overall approach and have some questions about this one item." "Explain to me more about what you mean here.")

· Personal, using "I" statements to express your point of view ("I have trouble when someone . . . , so I'd prefer if you . . ." "Instead of telling me . . . , I'd be more open if you asked me this way. . . .")

· Patient, without expecting the other person to comply instantly or change overnight ("I know it's going to take us time." "It's normal to have some ups and downs.")

· Open to the other person's feelings ("I can appreciate how angry you must feel." "I can see how upset you are; I'd be hurt, too.")

· An invitation to hear the other person's point of view ("What could we have done differently?" "What would work for you?")

· Careful to limit criticism to specific actions and not to the person's overall self-worth ("I still think you're a terrific . . . and what needs work is . . ." "I value you greatly as a partner, and that includes our ability to discuss these things.")

· Committed to cooperation and a positive outcome ("Since we both want . . . , we'll need to watch out for . . ." "How can we work better together?" "If we remember to . . . , we'll do fine.")

Receptive Listening

Quite often I hear people complain about a major aspect of this Achilles Heel: that their spouse, lover, parent, children, boss, or co-workers "don't listen" or "refuse to understand." We resent not being appreciated by those closest to us, yet we often don't see that they also need to be listened to and understood. The more you resist listening, the more they will persist in giving you what you don't want to hear. We all could use some improvement in learning to be more receptive and less reactive.

Each of us wants to be truly heard—to make sure another person understands exactly what we mean. When this doesn't happen, we feel misunderstood or neglected, and we tend to blame the listener. Yet communication often fails because we are so involved in protecting ourselves, controlling others, and proving we are "right."

Receptive listening breaks this pattern of miscommunication and accusation. It requires setting aside our own thoughts and feelings long enough to learn what the other person means, to actually feel what another feels. We need to listen beyond words to the sender's best intentions.

> *We resent not being appreciated by those closest to us, yet we often don't see that they also need to be listened to and understood. The more you resist listening, the more they will persist in giving you what you don't want to hear.*

Often it isn't criticism itself that gets us into trouble but our defensiveness. For example, if you can't stand your love partner criticizing you about a minor point, your refusal to listen will make the matter grow in importance and will push you further and further apart. If you bristle every time your boss looks over your shoulder, your productivity as well as your job satisfaction will suffer. If as a manager you aren't open to feedback from customers and employees, your effectiveness decreases.

Receptive listening is one of the most powerful means to communicate warmth and stimulate creativity. There are three components to receptive listening: developing empathy, shifting from "I'm right" to "point of view," and staying calm.

Developing Empathy

Empathy is defined in *Webster's New Collegiate Dictionary* as "the capacity for participation in another's feelings or ideas." With regard to hearing criticism, empathy means listening to other persons in such a way that you can understand the feelings beneath the words. It means striving to see their frame of reference, including how they perceive you and your actions. When you are giving criticism, empathy means being open to appreciating the other person's reasons and point of view. Instead of trying to convince people that they should feel different, empathy helps you seek to understand why they feel the way they do.

Just as you would not want to resist or argue when someone says, "I don't like spinach," so is it pointless to try to talk such individuals out of the way they feel about you. Rather than shouting, "You don't know what you're talking about, I'm not that way," you can save yourself a lot of trouble by asking them instead to tell you more. If you were in their shoes, you might feel the same way. Instead of viewing the other person as "wrong," you can learn what your behavior looks like from his or her frame of reference.

Even if other people are using destructive criticism ("You always do this." "You did it on purpose."), somewhere behind their use of guilt or intimidation is a clue to understanding them better. The trick is to find something constructive even when it is shrouded in destructive tactics. For example, if your parents often criticize you with manipulative tactics to get you to visit them more often, you don't have to defend yourself immediately or else comply with their wishes. When your mother or father says, "How come you never visit?" it is less an attack on your character than a clue to the needs and feelings of your aging parents. Instead of needing to justify yourself or immediately react with irritation, you can simply hear within their statement that they love and miss you. You might say in return that you love and miss them as well without needing to explain, defend, or comply.

The same principle applies with spouses or roommates who use criticism to manipulate or intimidate. If they are shouting, "I do all the dirty work. You never do anything around the house," you don't have to convince them that their feelings of working so hard are inaccurate. Having empathy means that you can appreciate that your spouse or roommate is feeling burdened. Ask for more input and show them you understand: "I agree you've been doing a lot around the house." That doesn't mean, however, that you must immediately haul out the garbage. Once you achieve understanding of what both of you want and need, then you can calmly develop solutions where both of you are satisfied.

Sometimes we fear that if we let them have their say, they'll think we are in complete agreement. This need not be the case. Let the other person know you've understood his or her criticism even if you're not ready or able to comply with it. When you give people the love and support of hearing them out, they can better understand your frame of reference.

From "I'm Right" to "Point of View"

Most arguments have little if anything to do with the words being used or the ideas being discussed. For instance, you and a loved one may quarrel over politics, women's rights, or your reactions to a recent film. The anger and heated words are often less about the issue and more about "who's right," who's in control, and who has the final authority.

We human beings are incredibly self-righteous: When giving or receiving criticism, we know how right we are and how wrong the other person is. Neither side wants to give in, and both sides feel misunderstood. We often create for ourselves a Greek chorus of like-minded friends and allies to reflect back to us how right we are and how wrong the other person is.

We human beings are incredibly self-righteous: When giving or receiving criticism, we know how right we are and how wrong the other person is.

When both sides are defending "I'm right and you're wrong" positions, you are no longer just discussing a specific criticism but are engaged in a struggle of wills. You may think you are arguing the merits of an issue, but you feel as if you are fighting for the survival of your self-worth and identity.

If you have a cherished belief that someone criticizes, you may react as if you yourself are being attacked. Even if you're being criticized for a self-destructive habit, such as smoking or repeatedly being late, it may feel as if your identity is under attack. The Achilles Syndrome has been activated: The more you react to criticism as an attack on your emotional survival, the more you will be blinded to the potential merits of the other person's point of view. When we perceive criticism as an accusation or putdown, we often defend against it as if our lives were at stake.

If we give up insisting how right we are and try to listen receptively, we allow the other person to be right as well. What you resist persists—the more you insist how wrong the other person is, the more he will persist in trying to prove how right he is. Focusing on "point of view" means learning that at any given moment each of us is right from his or her own perspective. When it comes to feelings, no one is wrong. A key to success in your business and personal relationships is to value and accept seemingly opposite points of view.

> ✗ Focusing on "point of view" means learning that at any given moment each of us is right from his or her own perspective. When it comes to feelings, no one is wrong.

Whether dealing with our loved ones or colleagues, here are some of the ways we indicate "I'm right and you're wrong":

- Showing impatience with everything that's said
- Frequently interrupting
- Never giving in, even if the other view makes sense
- Making others feel guilty, stupid, or awkward
- Fighting for your position as if your life depends on it

On the other hand, when we are listening receptively, our intention is that the other person feel more relaxed, appreciated, and understood. A receptive communication style involves:

- Giving someone your undivided attention without jumping to conclusions or planning your next move.
- Reflecting warmth in your body posture, eye contact, voice tone, and facial expressions.
- Asking thoughtful questions in order to understand their point of view better.
- Appreciating the feelings that underlie the words.
- Calmly reflecting back to them their feelings without adding on, judging, or attacking. If you can repeat their point of view using phrases like "I can see how ... ," "I understand how you feel ... ," or "I appreciate your saying ... ," the person criticizing you will be more likely to see your point of view as well.

Staying Calm

Most people feel tense and defensive under criticism. As soon as you notice your temperature rising and muscles tightening, the best thing to do is to stop and regain your sense of personal safety. Breathe a few deep inhales and exhales, sit quietly for a moment. When you take a few moments to regain your composure, the criticism almost always seems more benign.

In many instances someone may be criticizing you for reasons that have little to do with you. The cashier at the store may be irritable because he or she is having a bad day. You are not the primary cause of that person's sarcasm or anger. The same applies to your romantic partner, who may have gotten up on the wrong side of the bed. We've all been in those moods where we get critical with someone simply because they say, "Hi!"

Often we criticize in others the things we can't accept in ourselves. For instance, if your spouse or lover accuses you of being lazy or sloppy, there is a good chance your laziness or sloppiness has simply triggered their own disapproval of themselves. In essence they are saying, "How can I possibly tolerate in you what I criticize myself for all the time?"

Instead of getting angry or feeling put upon, seek to understand and empathize with what is bothering them. You may want to improve your habits or you may be satisfied that you are sufficiently hardworking and diligent. In either case, the more you can recognize when your partner is dealing with his or her own issues, the less likely you are to take it personally. Instead of reacting defensively with, "You're always so compulsive around the house," you might want to empathize with your partner by saying calmly, "A clean house is important to me also. Let's discuss what arrangement would be more satisfying for both of us."

If in spite of your intention to stay calm, you find yourself getting defensive when a loved one or associate is criticizing you, ask for a twenty-minute timeout. Your purpose is not to avoid a necessary discussion, but rather to take some time to reflect and regain your composure. You might want to say, "I'm not at my best right now. Let me take a few minutes for myself so that I can hear you better." In some cases you may want to think about the criticism overnight or until your next meeting. You have the right to say, "Thanks for your suggestions. Let me give them some thought, and I'll tell you what I need to put them into action." Since criticism often challenges some of our most cherished beliefs about ourselves, it is natural that you will need time to digest and integrate the person's advice.

> ✗ *Often we criticize in others the things we can't accept in ourselves.*

The Inner Critic

The way we respond to the criticism of others tells a great deal about how we feel about ourselves. If we are already plagued by self-criticism, we will be particularly troubled when we get criticism from others. Even if someone praises us and has only one small thing to criticize, we usually zero in on the inadequacy more than the things we did well.

For example, Brenda is a hardworking first-year attorney for a major law firm. She receives a lot of praise for her competence, yet all it takes is a senior partner pointing out a minor oversight and she feels her job, and more important her worth, are on the line. Brenda can't hear the slightest criticism without feeling overwhelmed by the harsh judgment of her own "inner critic."

Just as Achilles' mother wished her child to be perfect and invulnerable, so do many of us internalize inappropriate or excessively high parental expectations. Criticism and high hopes from our parents may have carried an extra sting because of our parents' inability to separate their own self-worth from the actions of their children. Getting a low grade in school was bad, but not half as bad as the disappointment it caused our parents. Getting divorced or losing a job may have been painful, yet not nearly as traumatic as informing our parents.

When I ask people to recall their parent's criticisms, they can often fill pages with examples such as the following:

- "We expect so much more from you because we know what you're capable of."
- "After all we've done for you . . ."
- "I'd rather die than let a child of mine . . ."
- "If you were more careful, this never would have happened."
- "You're wasting your talents."
- "You deserve someone so much better than that."
- "You're doing this to hurt us, aren't you?"

Many people criticize themselves worse than their parents ever did. Children of especially demanding parents internalize high expectations that stay with them long after they leave their parents' home. Any insecurity, weakness, or problem area in your life may cause you to hear the echoes of your parents' disappointment: "How could this be happening to our son (daughter)?" "Where did we go wrong?" "If you loved us, you wouldn't be acting this way." Under the pressure of always acting like a "good boy" or "good girl," you may have worried that any selfishness on your part might cause your parents to reject you. You learned to do everything in your power to hold back what was unacceptable. *Especially if your parents said, "Why can't you be like . . . ," you may have learned to suppress your uniqueness in favor of becoming a second-rate imitation of the person your parents wanted you to be.*

> ✗. *Many people criticize themselves worse than their parents ever did.*

Overcoming the Approval Trap

Dorothy's case is a good illustration of how our "inner critic" can expose our Achilles Heel and make us extra-sensitive to criticism. Dorothy is a thirty-six-year-old executive secretary for a stock brokerage firm. She also cooks and cleans for her husband and two teenage sons. In spite of wearing both hats as a housewife and working mother, Dorothy never feels she is doing enough. When one of her sons was having trouble in school, Dorothy felt personally at fault for not helping him more with his homework. When she had to stay home from work with the flu, she felt guilty about letting her co-workers down. She is so hard on herself that when her husband, Gene, says, "Dorothy, did you call the man about the air-conditioning?" she becomes alarmed. When her children don't clean up their room, rather than risk "back talk," she simply does it for them. Finally, one evening her mother-in-law criticized Dorothy's new couch and drapes; Dorothy became so frustrated, she decided to come for therapy.

During her first visit she told me, "No matter how hard I try, someone is always finding fault. I feel like I just can't win with Gene, the kids, and especially my mother-in-law." Like many of us, Dorothy was feeling caught in the "approval trap": The harder she tried to make other people happy, the more unhappy she felt when they were still dissatisfied.

I explained to Dorothy, "We all want unconditional love, to be appreciated free of demands or expectations. Yet all growth involves the integration of seemingly opposite values—the paradox of unconditional love is accepting that we all have conditions. No one in the history of the world has ever won a 100-percent popularity contest, not even Jesus Christ, Albert Schweitzer, or Mother Theresa. No matter how much you do for others, some people will still criticize, complain, or have tastes that differ from your own. What makes you think you can please everyone?"

> *All growth involves the integration of seemingly opposite values— the paradox of unconditional love is accepting that we all have conditions.*

There is no shortage in this life of unsolicited opinions, criticism, and advice. The trick is to learn to hear without discomfort and to evaluate it without necessarily acting on it.

To assist Dorothy in overcoming the "approval trap," I suggested as a homework assignment that she make a list of the *should*s that kept her feeling inadequate and immobilized. Among the items on Dorothy's list were the following:

- "A good mother should always be at home for her children."
- "A good wife should be more cheerful."
- "A real lady should never get angry."
- "I should never talk back to my mother-in-law."
- "You should respect your elders."
- "I should be more flexible to accommodate other people's needs."

While none of these *should*s is right or wrong per se, putting such heavy emphasis on demands and expectations makes us feel less alive and energetic. Since Dorothy thought she had no right to talk back to her mother-in-law, she was left feeling defenseless and victimized. As part of her therapy I encouraged Dorothy to express her anger to me in a role-playing exercise as if I were her mother-in-law. At first Dorothy held back, saying, "I can't raise my voice to my mother-in-law," but when she understood that she could use this exercise to avoid a destructive confrontation with her mother-in-law, she really got involved. Shaking a fist, Dorothy hurled an angry tirade at me as I played her mother-in-law. She shouted such things as follows:

- "Nobody likes you; your taste is just horrible."
- "You're always breathing down my neck and finding fault."
- "You never liked me from the start."

- "Leave me alone and stop trying to undermine my marriage."
- "I'm different from you. Quit telling me how to run my life."
- "I hate it when you criticize me."

Note that acting out your anger in a role-playing exercise does not mean you should make destructive comments to the actual person. Under no circumstances should you use the insights from this helpful exercise as ammunition with which to get back at someone. Just as it's dangerous to err on the side of being too compliant, so is it harmful just to ventilate your rage at the person. Dealing with a difficult relative requires integrating assertiveness with understanding: a commitment not to being "right" but to being effective. You must stand up for your rights while respecting the other person's need to feel respected.

> ✗ *"Dealing with a difficult relative requires integrating assertiveness with understanding: a commitment not to being "right" but to being effective. You must stand up for your rights while respecting the other person's need to feel respected.*

Once Dorothy had safely let off steam, I suggested we switch roles, with Dorothy playing her mother-in-law and me as Dorothy. I initiated the following dialogue to show

Dorothy how to deal more effectively with her mother-in-law's criticism:

DOROTHY: (played by me)	Could we please talk? I've got something important I want to share with you.
MOTHER-IN-LAW: (played by Dorothy)	If that's what you want, then go ahead.
DOROTHY:	I was uncomfortable with our discussion the other day about my new couch and drapes.
MOTHER-IN-LAW:	Oh? You shouldn't be so sensitive. You just don't know as much about picking quality as I do.
DOROTHY:	You certainly can have your own opinion, but I have a right to my own taste in choosing things for the house.
MOTHER-IN-LAW:	Of course it's your decision, but you've got to admit the design on the drapes doesn't go with the couch. I'm sure Gene would agree it just has to go back.
DOROTHY:	Actually, Gene and I have talked it over, and we very much like the drapes and couch. What's more important, though, is to recognize that I love you and we have different tastes. In your home I appreciate your tastes and I hope that in my home you'll respect mine.

MOTHER-IN-LAW:	Okay, but I don't think you care one bit about what I have to offer.
DOROTHY:	I sincerely appreciate how much you do. Baby-sitting the kids whenever Gene and I go out of town, teaching me your best recipes, and of course your wonderful dinner parties. I want you to know I appreciate and love you even when we disagree.
MOTHER-IN-LAW:	You do?
DOROTHY:	Absolutely. Even when I do things the opposite of what you'd like, I still very much care about and love you.

Instead of stifling your anger, the key is to practice channeling it into constructive criticism. While miraculous changes won't happen overnight, favoring the positive can significantly improve even your most difficult relationship. Two days after our practice session, Dorothy had a successful heart-to-heart talk with her mother-in-law. From then on, rather than feeling devastated every time her mother-in-law criticized her, Dorothy could set firm but gentle limits. For example, instead of feeling she "had to" cook dinner for her mother-in-law once a week, Dorothy suggested they go to a restaurant more often (where her mother-in-law could criticize the waitress instead of Dorothy).

The more Dorothy learned to deal with her "inner critic," the easier it was for her to accept that her husband, children, and in-laws had some reasonable as well as some unreasonable expectations of her that she herself had cultivated. Dorothy began to lighten her load as a working mother by encouraging her husband and children to become more responsible for cleaning up after themselves. One of the great lessons of life is to be able to say no as well as yes to those we love and work with.

The *"I Can't Stand Criticism"* Couple

Giving and receiving criticism effectively is essential to a healthy love relationship. When two people fall in love, they open to each other the most sensitive parts of their personalities. Love, by its very nature, creates occasions for disappointment and consequently for criticism. All love relationships are to some extent ambivalent—we love and often feel most critical of those with whom we are closest. In any long-term relationship, there will inevitably be times when the partners infuriate each other or are insensitive to each other's feelings. The irony of love is that it guarantees some degree of anger, frustration, and criticism.

> *The irony of love is that it guarantees some degree of anger, frustration, and criticism.*

Many couples make the mistake of believing they can protect their relationship either by being extra-critical of each other or by never criticizing each other at all. When criticism is used in excess, both love partners are essentially saying, "I love the person I'm hoping to change you into," which implies, "I don't love you the way you are." The more you resist your partner as he or she is and use criticism to manipulate or control, the more your partner will persist in doing the things that irritate you. As we saw earlier, we often mistake criticism for a threat to our survival. In a relationship in which one or both partners are extremely critical, both partners may feel as though they are fighting for their emotional survival.

The more common situation is when both partners have an unwritten contract that says, "I won't criticize you if you won't criticize me." Significant incidents and irritations are ignored. Things that you would like to change are covered up with rationalizations like "It's not important" or "We'll deal with this later." Both partners are terrified that bringing up any criticism at all will disrupt the harmony of the relationship. Pretty soon unresolved hurts and resentments begin to surface in destructive ways.

> *When criticism is used in excess, both love partners are essentially saying, "I love the person I'm hoping to change you into," which implies, "I don't love you the way you are."*

A relationship remains free from a buildup of resentments only if both partners can share constructive criticism. This does not mean picking at your partner for every small detail and minor irritation. But one of the greatest gifts you can give the people you love is to hear their anger and frustration without judging or contradicting them. We can feel most loved when someone accepts our anger and empathizes with our hurt feelings. The closer you are to someone, the more skilled you must be at knowing when to argue and when simply to hold your partner and say, "I understand."

In a relationship in which both partners have the interlocking Achilles Heels of "I can't stand criticism," there is
no outlet for expressing the irritations and upsets that occur
from time to time. When criticism remains repressed, it
builds up until there's a destructive explosion or, worse, a
gradual erosion of love through hurt silences and sarcastic
sniping. Expressing criticism is crucial to sustaining a passionate sexual interest. Not that love is a license to criticize
indiscriminately, but couples with boring sex lives are often
the ones that claim they never fight. Instead they become
"emotionally constipated." Repressed anger blocks the sexual chemistry as "never fight" becomes "never make love."

> ✎ *One of the greatest gifts you can
> give the people you love is to hear their
> anger and frustration without judging
> or contradicting them.*

For example, Jeff is a real estate developer and his wife,
Bonnie, is a sales representative for a computer firm. After
four years of marriage, they have what all their friends and
relatives consider an "ideal marriage." They have exciting
careers, a lovely home, and a bright future. Yet they came
to my office for a consultation because, "We rarely make
love anymore."

Neither Jeff nor Bonnie could understand why their sex
life had become so boring. They talked about how much
they love each other, what they do for each other, and how
much fun they have on weekends and vacations. They both
felt technically proficient at lovemaking. As Bonnie admit-

ted, "It's not a matter of reading another sex manual—we've practically read them all."

I got a clue about their sexual apathy when they said, "We never fight." When we explored the conflicts in their relationship, I found that many frustrations and potential criticisms were never expressed because both partners live by the principle of "If you have nothing nice to say, say nothing at all." Jeff was irritated whenever Bonnie called to say she would be late for dinner. Bonnie resented Jeff's attitude that because his income was larger, he had more to say about financial matters. Jeff never told Bonnie how annoyed he had been when she had flirted with his business partner at an important dinner. Bonnie never told Jeff how much she felt let down when he didn't want to go along to visit her parents. The list goes on, minor irritations spliced with major misunderstandings. All are denied in the hope that the resentments will somehow go away. They don't. Passion does.

Jeff and Bonnie feared that if they criticized or argued with each other, their relationship would be filled with friction. Both of them had childhood memories of bitter fights between their own parents and were afraid of slipping into that kind of behavior themselves. They needed to experience firsthand that lovers can criticize each other without lingering hostility. Jeff and Bonnie needed to learn the art of constructive criticism.

I instructed them in a "Tell Me More" exercise that can be used whenever you and your partner need to clear up a misunderstanding. Jeff and Bonnie took the phone off the hook and then sat closely, facing each other. The guidelines of "Tell Me More" are as follows:

1. Each person begins by affirming his or her commitment to love and a positive outcome by stating,

"Out of the love I have for you and out of the love I know you have for me, there are a few specific things we need to clean up."

2. One person speaks at a time and is never interrupted except for an occasional and encouraging "Tell me more."

3. Communications are specific, empathic, and nonjudgmental. Words like *always*, *never*, and *should* are to be avoided.

4. Each specific criticism must be delivered briefly in two or three sentences. No monologues are allowed.

5. Both partners are to maintain eye contact, take deep breaths, and remain calm.

6. After each person speaks, the listener must restate what was said without judging, defending, or "adding on." This is to make sure that what you think you heard is actually what the speaker intended. By offering "What I hear you saying is . . . ," you can clarify what the other person meant.

7. Once the first speaker's message is clearly understood, it's time to switch. The partner who was the listener now has a chance to be the speaker, while the other person listens and says only, "Tell me more." Ample time must be set aside so that both sides can express their feelings without interference.

8. Especially for couples, it is helpful at the end of this exercise to hug and say, "I love you." Remember that one of the greatest gifts you can give someone you love is to hear his or her anger and

frustration without judging, getting defensive, or contradicting.

The goal of the "Tell Me More" exercise is to keep clarifying the other person's feelings and intentions until you know what it's like to be inside each other's experience. This simple but profound technique can raise the quality of a marriage or any intimate relationship.

The "Tell Me More" exercise is not a disguised license to badger, complain, or manipulate, but rather a way to bring people closer together. Jeff and Bonnie used the exercise not to pick at each other but to be genuinely constructive about how to improve their sex life. It was the first time either had the freedom to explore in detail what they missed and what they enjoyed about sex. Jeff began by telling Bonnie how rejected and insecure he felt whenever he wanted to make love and she didn't. Bonnie restated Jeff's feelings, and it was clear she appreciated how difficult it was for him to have to be the initiator most of the time. Then Bonnie explained her fear that any "bedroom criticism" would hurt Jeff and "turn him off." Without adding on or analyzing, Jeff restated her feelings.

Jeff and Bonnie began to see their sexual "problem" as something they both shared and now wanted to solve. At this point, before any solutions had been offered, they were already feeling much closer and even more passionate. Their ability to clear the air, express feelings they had been withholding, and tell the truth was already very healing. Being allowed to express criticism had opened up a rich source of deep, positive feelings. As they continued the "Tell Me More" exercise by offering specific solutions, Jeff and Bonnie found new energy to restore the passion in their relationship.

Dealing With a Critical Boss

Criticism from a boss can be the cause of joyless workdays, bitter arguments, and a blow to your self-esteem. When you get "called on the carpet," you may feel like quitting, crying, or else getting even. In a work setting where criticism reigns, everyone feels threatened and therefore stuck in the Achilles Syndrome, performs less effectively.

Dealing with an especially critical or demanding boss is not easy. If your boss is in the habit of breathing down your neck or throwing fits, what options do you have? Most of us smile compliantly at our bosses while seething inside. Some employees fantasize about how great life would be if only they could fire their boss, change jobs, or quit.

Responding to a super-critical boss once again raises the important issue of "what you resist persists." The more you try to comply with or disobey a critical boss, the more he or she will grate on your nerves. Even if you go out of your way to make sure every little detail is perfect, a super-critical boss will find something to criticize.

> *In a work setting where criticism reigns, everyone feels threatened and therefore performs less effectively.*

The issue is not how to avoid criticism. In fact, many bosses think it is their job to find something to criticize. In some situations, you may be an unfair victim of office politics. You might get criticized simply because the guilty party is absent or is immune to criticism as a result of his or her rank or relationship to the president of the company. Sometimes you may feel unfairly blamed for the inadequacies of a product or management policy. Your boss may need to let off steam and you just happen to be the person within shouting distance.

Criticism is bound to be a part of any job; the key is learning to respond effectively. Here are some points to keep in mind when dealing with a critical boss:

- *Don't make a globally negative judgment about your competence based on an honest mistake.* Learn from your mistakes rather than pass the buck. If there were contributing problems outside your control, describe these realistically without making excuses.

- *Your boss will respect you for taking responsibility for losses as well as victories.* Rather than dumping the problem in your boss's lap or finding scapegoats to blame, take the initiative to find well-planned, creative alternatives. Instead of becoming defensive, help your boss find a workable solution.

- *Timing is important.* If your boss had just received news of the loss of a major contract or source of revenue, give him or her time to ventilate frustration and anger. Don't take personally anything your boss says in a fit of rage. Instead you might try to understand and empathize with your boss's feelings.

- *Don't be a pushover.* The meek shall inherit the earth, but only by becoming more assertive. The more you are seen as someone who provides a valuable service but who can't be pushed around, the less likely you will be a scapegoat in office politics.

You will be rewarded only if you know your just due and can ask for it.

Vivian's case is a good illustration of how to overcome a difficult situation with a highly critical boss. An assistant to a hard-driving vice-president of marketing, Vivian came for counseling after attending one of my corporate seminars Vivian reported, "My boss never lets up. He's always got ten things going at once and he expects me to jump through hoops every time he shouts for help. All it takes is one foul-up on my part and I hear about it for weeks."

> ✗ *The meek shall inherit the earth, but only by becoming more assertive. You will be rewarded only if you know your just due and can ask for it.*

Vivian thought she had reached her breaking point when her boss called her at home on a Saturday at 7:00 A.M. to demand that she fly immediately to represent the firm at a trade fair in Houston. As Vivian described to me in desperation, "My boss expects me to drop everything to go down there immediately and set up for the trade fair. I've got house guests coming from out of town. What am I going to do?"

Vivian needed to deal with her boss in an effective and professional manner. I gave her a series of guidelines to use when a boss makes unreasonable demands. Instead of feeling victimized, you can preserve your sanity and add to your worth as an employee by following the following principles:

• *Support your boss by acknowledging the importance of the situation.* Instead of trying to talk your boss out of what he or she thinks is so important, you can remain an ally by verbally acknowledging your boss's concerns. When Vivian called her boss back, the first thing she said was, "I agree that it's very important that we're represented well at the trade fair." Your boss has great pressures and can benefit enormously from a receptive ear.

• *Make your "no" firm, specific, and unequivocal.* Even though you are agreeing with your boss's concerns, you need not comply with an unreasonable demand. So Vivian continued, "And there's no way I can go to Houston, since I have out-of-town guests this weekend. With more notice I would have been happy to do it." Note that if Vivian had said, "Maybe," "I'll try," or "I'll see what I can do," she would probably have wound up in Houston feeling very resentful. Make your situation clear by relating the reasons why you must say no.

• *Offer suggestions without making unrealistic promises.* To demonstrate both her loyalty and professionalism further, Vivian concluded her phone call by saying, "I'm going to call one of our best contacts in Houston and see if she can cover for us. I'll get back to you within a half hour to tell you if I could reach her and if she can do it." Once again, Vivian didn't resist her boss's concerns but rather demonstrated that she is a valuable employee even when saying no to his demands.

Instead of offering herself as doormat her boss could walk over, Vivian showed him that she could be decisive and firm in a tough situation. In the long

run, her employer would treat her with more respect
for her constructive no than for being a "good girl"
who jumps at his beck and call. Instead of feeling
guilty for standing up for herself, Vivian felt good
about the way she handled her boss's demand. So
apparently did Vivian's boss; six months later she
was promoted.

In order to deal successfully with a critical boss, you will
invariably need to distinguish your boss's demands from
your own inner critic. A boss's criticisms or demands may
be minor compared with the pressures and insecurities you
heap upon yourself. Instead of becoming overly defensive
or compliant when your boss makes an unreasonable demand
or points out a minor error, take a few moments to ask
yourself the following questions:

- Am I being harder on myself than is necessary?
- Do I need to be so defensive, or is my boss trusting
  that I have the situation under control?
- Can I continue to feel good for all I'm doing right
  while correcting this mistake?
- Can I forgive myself for not being perfect and learn
  fully from this situation?

The sooner you can stop beating yourself up for a minor
error, the sooner your boss's criticism will cease to burden
you. With high self-esteem, you will feel better, and your
performance will improve. Becoming your own best boss
means being open to feedback and feeling good about your
competence even as you learn from your mistakes.

Favoring the Positive

One of the best ways to deal with this Achilles Heel is to remember that, whether at work or at home, criticism is always more effective when coupled with praise and support. It's far more valuable to catch your spouse, children, co-workers, and especially yourself doing something right than to catch them doing something wrong. Consider the following guidelines:

- *Don't forget to acknowledge yourself and others for being receptive to criticism.* Since criticism is difficult for most of us, learning to take criticism requires changing a number of old habits. Just like learning a new serve in tennis, for example, you must notice each small step of improvement. Every time you are less defensive or reactive when you are criticized, give yourself a pat on the back. Acknowledge your spouse, children, or co-workers when they respond well to criticism. None of us changes overnight, yet we feel encouraged when someone notices our signs of progress.

- *When it comes to criticism, "an ounce of prevention is worth a pound of cure."* Seek out feedback and further clarification *before* a miscommunication turns into a crisis. For example, when your boss asks for a report, you can save both of you much time and aggravation by finding out exactly what he or she wants in the first place. Instead of relying on vague assumptions with your love partner or guessing what he or she needs, ask for clarification and suggestions.

· *You have tremendous influence on the type of criticism you receive.* When you become more supportive and skillful at criticizing constructively, your loved ones and co-workers are sure to notice. Nothing begets appreciation like appreciation. Even when you are under fire, common courtesy can often turn the situation around. Rather than responding angrily, genuine friendliness, concern, and compassion can be disarming. How you treat others will also help them see how you want to be treated. If your criticism of them is brief, specific, and loving, they will gradually (not overnight!) learn to return the favor.

· *Learning to give constructive criticism must also paradoxically include being less critical.* There is an art to learning to accept yourself and others exactly the way you are without expecting miraculous changes. The less rejecting and intolerant you are, the better others can hear and use your criticism. Instead of always scolding and reprimanding others, it's okay to let some things slide and to focus only on those issues that really matter. For example, if you are the parent of teenagers, it's best not to waste your energy criticizing things like haircuts and clothes. You want to be sure that when the big issues, such as drugs, come up, there will still be enough rapport that your children will listen. When loved ones know you appreciate them and judge them fairly, they are more likely to value your suggestions.

· *Five specific acknowledgments a day keeps the critic away.* Especially in our intimate relationships, we need to feel loved and appreciated. For a couple that has fallen into the habit of criticizing too much or taking each other for granted, a good exercise is for each of you to list on a piece of paper five specific things you like about the other. Items must be positive and specific. Take a moment to tell him or her how much you appreciate the conversation you had while walking through the park. When a song or a memory makes you recall how much you enjoy your partner, make sure you let the other person know. Compliment a hairdo or new outfit. Find the opportunity to give specific positive and loving feedback each day, no matter how long you've been together.

· *Super-critical people may be crying out for love and appreciation.* Instead of criticizing them for criticizing you, find out what such people are asking for. Underneath anger there is usually hurt. Acknowledging a difficult person breaks the tension between you. Instead of putting up defenses or trying to get back at them, you might soften their blows by empathizing with their feelings. A smile or kind word is often more potent than a hostile reply.

· *Remember you are bigger than the event or trait for which you are being criticized.* Just as your Achilles Heel is only a small part of your personality, a criticism is a statement about a behavior and not about your entire worth. It is easier not to become defensive if you keep this in mind. In spite of what you may have been told as a child, you deserve to be loved even when you make mistakes or have difficulties. Seeing criticism as helpful feedback allows you to use it for growth rather than as a devastating exposé of your shortcomings.

5. Making Peace With Time: "I'm Always Feeling Tense and Rushed"

Is your internal motor running faster than the world around you? You're impatient waiting for your instant coffee machine to boil. The transit system is running a half hour late. Airline Reservations has you on hold, with the dentist-office music grating on your nerves. The growth stock you purchased moved like a centipede. The avocado you bought last Tuesday still hasn't ripened. To top it off, your luncheon date shows up an hour late, and on the way back from lunch you find the automatic teller machine is out of order and the bank clerk needs two approvals to cash your check. Most people would gladly become less tense and rushed—if only they had the time!

In our fast-paced, "I want it done yesterday" world, in which change and frenzy seem to be the one constants, you may feel like a car barreling out of control down a narrow mountain highway. How are you supposed to enjoy the ride or appreciate the scenery when you are in constant danger of losing your grip and crashing down a steep drop? What is all this tension and rushing for? For many, it is to be able to afford a first heart attack, divorce, and psychotherapy for their children.

> *Most people would gladly become less tense and rushed—if only they had the time!*

Most of us take on more than it is humanly possible to accomplish in any given day. Handling innumerable chores and crises at home, work, and in transit while also trying to pack in athletics, social activities, and fun, we hardly find time to come up for air. Sooner or later, as we try to cram more and more things into less and less time, the body rebels. Human beings don't "suddenly" develop a heart attack or ulcers. By the time serious illness strikes, there have been years of neglected clues to slow down, reexamine priorities, and listen to your body's signals.

The danger of the Achilles Heel of "I'm always feeling tense and rushed" is that it is so common and becomes so familiar that you barely recognize how burnt out you are. You're so used to being under pressure, you don't remember what it's like to relax. Inactivity is what seems unpleasant or threatening to you. You try resting, but your mind still races with things to do. You take a few moments of quiet with your family, and immediately an argument ensues. You take a day off from work and spend the entire time catching up on errands and chores. You have difficulty sleeping because you worry about your love life or work.

You may try to appear calm when you're under the gun, but your body knows the difference. Feigning tranquillity doesn't take the pressure off. Check to see if you have any of the following signs and symptoms of feeling chronically tense and rushed:

- Taking on more when you are already overscheduled
- Feeling guilty relaxing if there's work to be done
- Feeling irritated by the shortcomings or demands of others
- Competing to show who's a harder worker
- Worrying when you have to delegate responsibility or ask for assistance
- Fearing your success is due to speed and hard work rather than insight and creativity
- Becoming upset when you have to wait on line
- Wondering if people love you not for who you are but for what you do
- Suffering from heartburn, tension headaches, or muscle spasms
- Noticing what you fail to do instead of what you accomplish

> *Human beings don't "suddenly" develop a heart attack or ulcers. By the time serious illness strikes, there have been years of neglected clues to slow down, reexamine priorities, and listen to your body's signals.*

In addition, try this simple test to see whether you suffer from the Achilles Heel of being tense and rushed. Take an uninterrupted five minutes to sit comfortably, close your eyes, and let yourself relax. This is a time for idle enjoyment. If you open your eyes and see by your watch that the five minutes aren't over, close your eyes again and continue the test. *Now do this exercise before reading any further.*

Done? What happened? Did you find that the five minutes passed quickly or slowly? Were you mostly anxious, bored, and annoyed or calm and comfortable? The experience of time is highly variable. Though it is a cliché, time *does* seem to fly when we're enjoying ourselves and to crawl when we have to do something unpleasant.

If you're like most people, the five minutes passed slowly and you felt bored and restless. Perhaps your mind was filled with thoughts of all the things you have done or need to do. Perhaps you noticed some tension in your shoulders and neck. Perhaps you started worrying or feeling angry about what appeared to be a waste of time. These are all signals of tension and pressure.

Pressured for Time

We most often feel tense and rushed when we are dealing with being late. Have you been stuck in traffic inhaling exhaust fumes, your mind and blood pressure racing? Have you waited on a crowded train or subway platform feeling like you're never going to reach your destination? Did you use these opportunities to relax, listen to music, or daydream about your favorite adventure? Or did you do what most people do—berate yourself for not leaving earlier or rage bitterly against the "stupid" drivers all around you or the failing transit system?

If you are frequently late for appointments, you may spend much of your time not only racing the clock but trying desperately to come up with excuses. Arriving at your appointed destination doesn't reduce the tension. You then have to face the dirty looks, snide comments, and skeptical reactions that follow your lengthy explanations.

Looking back over your career as a late person, can you recall the lovers who took your lateness personally, the employers who threatened or fired you, the movies and plays of which you never saw the opening scenes? How about those unforgettable times when someone found a hole in your carefully prepared story and stared right through you? In spite of what your lateness has cost, it's been hard to give it up. Perhaps you see it as your trademark, one of the ways you identify yourself.

This Achilles Heel, which makes time so difficult to deal with, has another side: You may be someone who is rarely late, but who frequently finds yourself waiting. You rush to arrive on schedule, often get there ahead of time, and then do a slow boil as you wait. You glance at your watch wondering whether to leave, lecture the culprit on human decency, or simply smile and say, "No problem." Needing always to be on time can cause as much tension as always being late.

> *Looking back over your career as a late person, can you recall the lovers who took your lateness personally, the employers who threatened or fired you, the movies and plays of which you never saw the opening scenes?*

The Fate of Ms. Late and Mr. I-Hate-to-Wait

I saw a couple in counseling who had the interlocking Achilles Heels of one partner being chronically late while the other was obsessively punctual. Laura and Phil, both in their late thirties, had been introduced by close friends and found themselves immediately attracted to each other. Laura is a talented painter whose work has been shown in several exhibits. Phil is an accountant who specializes in representing recording artists and movie stars. They make an attractive couple, Phil's conservative suits and blond chiseled features contrasting with Laura's exotic outfits and brunette, waist-length hair. After six months of dating, they began making plans to live together and possibly get married.

While they are very compatible in the areas of sexuality, money, and shared interests, Phil and Laura fight frequently over her lateness versus his impatience. The more Phil criticizes and gives advice, the more agitated and also late Laura becomes. The more she is behind schedule, the more he grows short-tempered. A typical example occurred when Laura was to meet Phil at a reception for his most important client at seven o'clock. Here is what happened:

Mr. I-Hate-to-Wait	Ms. Late
4:00 P.M. Rushing between meetings, he calls Laura to make sure she'll be on time. No answer.	Shopping for painting supplies, she stops into a gallery to admire some silk screens by an unknown artist.

Mr. I-Hate-to-Wait	Ms. Late
5:00 P.M. Following a heated argument with a producer, Phil calls Laura. Again no answer. He's starting to become upset.	Leaving the gallery, she has an idea for a series of murals, which she sketches in her journal.
6:00 P.M. He finds out that the caterer delivered goose pâté and the guest of honor is vegetarian. Phil calls Laura; no answer. Then he calls the caterer and demands that they send vegetable pâté immediately.	She stops for gas on the way home because the tank was below empty; she wants to be sure not to be late for the reception.
6:15 P.M. He finally reaches Laura. Even though he tries to be calm, he finds himself interrogating her: "Where were you?" "Did you forget?" "Why aren't you dressed yet?"	She feels attacked and belittled by his questions. If only he'd stop yelling at her and let her get dressed, she wouldn't run late.
6:25 P.M. Phil gets a phone call from the caterer that says they're out of vegetable pâté. Will quiche do?	She doesn't dry off thoroughly from her quick shower and gets her favorite blouse wet. Now what to wear?
6:35 P.M. Phil calls to apologize for being so abrasive, and finds Laura to be sarcastic and preoccupied.	Trying to talk on the phone and put on makeup at the same time, Laura smudges her eyeliner. She must start over.

Mr. I-Hate-to-Wait	*Ms. Late*
6:45 P.M. Phil is pacing his office, wondering why he ever got involved with someone so inconsiderate.	Laura leaves the house, wondering why she ever got involved with someone so high-pressured.
6:55 P.M. Phil is popping antacids in his mouth when his guest of honor calls to say he will be late.	Laura rushes back into the house because she forgot to transfer her wallet and driver's license into her other purse.
7:15 P.M. The guests finally begin to arrive and Phil pretends to be gracious and in control.	Laura is stuck in traffic and trying to decide whether to tell Phil about her ideas for a new set of murals—or tell him to go to hell.
7:35 P.M. Phil greets his guest of honor, who is closely followed by an impeccable and aloof-looking Laura.	Laura and Phil give each other a kiss that misses by three inches. They barely speak to each other the rest of the evening.

(NOTE: While in this example Laura is late and Phil is impatient, as a general rule both men and women equally share the traits of lateness and impatience.)

In counseling, I asked Laura and Phil to examine how much they each took the other's actions as a personal affront. Phil was sure that Laura's lateness showed a complete disregard for his feelings and a lack of respect. Laura had serious questions about Phil's hostility and his lack of serious interest in her art career. His position was, "If you cared enough about me, you'd make a point to be on time." Her position was, "If you cared enough about me, you'd be less uptight and more understanding." It was a no-win situation: Both felt victimized and unappreciated.

I suggested to them that being late or impatient aggravated each other's Achilles Heels. The more you try to prove how wrong the other person is—in terms of either lateness or impatience—the more the other person needs to persist in proving how right he or she is. The issue is not who's right and who's wrong, but what hidden motivations may lie behind the lateness or impatience.

> ✂ *The more you try to prove how wrong the other person is—in terms of either lateness or impatience—the more the other person needs to persist in proving how right he or she is.*

I suggested to Phil and Laura that instead of blaming each other, they start learning more about themselves and each other. Which of these following common but often hidden motivations apply to you:

Hidden Motivations for Being Chronically Late

- *A test of loyalty.* By showing up late, you may be trying to discover how important you are to other people. Will they wait for me? Will they still love me? Will they accept and understand my excuses? If you were more certain of your worth, you wouldn't need to put others through these tests.

- *Defiance.* Even though Phil and Laura love each other, they both have staunchly independent personalities. Laura's lateness has always been her trademark and way of defying authority—which has unfortunately carried over into their current relationship. It's her way of showing she's "above the rules." For Laura that's part of her artistic temperament. For others it may be a way of telling you they're interested in more important things while you're involved in "silly details."

- *Attention-seeking*. By showing up late, Laura wins the spotlight and makes a grand entrance. This can be a kind of arrogant rebuttal, as if to say, "See, hasn't it all been worth it?"

- *One-upmanship*. Always being the one who's late may be a way of saying, "*I'm* the one people wait for. No one else is important enough for me to wait for."

- *A cherished habit*. Since Laura has been chronically late for much of her life, to give it up would mean forcing herself not only to learn a new habit but to look more deeply at what makes her unique. Holding on to chronic lateness is sometimes like holding on to a childlike, spontaneous part of ourselves we are afraid to lose.

- *Revenge*. Rather than giving in to an angry person who is forever breathing down your neck, you may secretly be getting back at him or her by being late.

- *Self-defeat*. Showing up late is the surest way to miss out on opportunities. If you secretly fear failure or rejection, your lateness can be a smokescreen. By missing important deadlines or forgetting a loved one's birthday, you may be setting yourself up for failure in your love life and career.

• *Stress addiction*. If you always seem to be running late, you may be addicted to the adrenaline surge of feeling rushed. Laura felt more creative under pressure, whereas being early or on time was "a little boring."

• *Bad judgment*. Quite simply, lateness is often an unwillingness to set priorities and leave enough time for what's important. Laura needed to build into her schedule more leeway and recognize that "something will always come up."

• *Hating to wait*. Many latecomers can't stand to be kept waiting and thus make others wait instead.

> ✗ *If you always seem to be running late, you may be addicted to the adrenaline surge of feeling rushed.*

Hidden Motivations for Being Chronically Impatient

• *A need to ventilate*. If you are in a business in which you sometimes have to swallow your anger, blowing up at a loved one for making you wait may be a search for a safer outlet. In Phil's case, he was failing to deal with minor irritations as they came up (vegetable pâté versus quiche and a guest of honor who calls at the last minute to say he'll be late). He blew up at Laura not only because her lateness was irritating but because of several other factors that weren't her fault.

- *Power plays*. When you act self-righteous and intolerant of other people's lateness, you are probably secretly expecting they will apologize and make it up to you. Yet the more you resist people's chronic lateness, the less attention they will pay to your lecturing and advice. When you treat someone like a naughty child, you may be inadvertently encouraging him or her to remain that way. There's nothing wrong with setting limits about how long you'll wait. The trick is to do it without causing yourself—or the other person—unnecessary pain.

- *A test of virtue*. Being compulsively early may be a way of proving that you are more virtuous and proper than others. Expecting others to be early becomes a kind of moral test.

- *Stress addiction*. If being tense and rushed is far more familiar to you than being relaxed, you may be seeking reasons to justify your impatience. You may feel comfortable only when you are pressured and angry—and blaming someone else for causing you to be that way.

- *A fear of being controlled*. Rather than accepting other people's lateness for what it is—their own problem that you need not take personally—many of us fear that if we let them get away with being late, it will encourage them to control us in other ways. For example, Phil was both in awe of and somewhat intimidated by Laura's impulsiveness and creativity. Phil and Laura were engaged in a struggle for control between her spontaneity and his orderliness.

· *Revenge*. In resorting to pouts, an angry look, or shouting, you may be using your impatience to strike back at the other person for making you feel unappreciated at other, unrelated times. You may be acting out some leftover bitterness from unspoken resentments in your sex life or as a carryover from previous relationships.

· *Intimidation*. You can use impatience to manipulate others. You can use it to tell them what to do, when to do it, and how much time it should take. By your impatience you hope to demonstrate that your life and priorities are much more significant than theirs.

✗. *If being tense and rushed is far more familiar to you than being relaxed, you may feel comfortable only when you are pressured and angry— and blaming someone else for causing you to be that way.*

· *Testing*. If someone does not show up on time, you can use that to get you out of a relationship you aren't 100 percent comfortable in. You judge your romantic partner's love or your business partner's dependability on whether he or she is prompt and enthusiastic, when in fact there are deeper concerns you are afraid to articulate. If you put your relationship on the line every time someone is late, no wonder you are so pained by your impatience.

- *Unclear priorities*. If you aren't sure in the first place whether you want to be somewhere and then the other person shows up late, you may be extra miffed. Your irritation may be more with yourself for agreeing to do something your common sense told you to avoid. Instead of blaming the latecomer, you may want to become more assertive about not committing yourself to things you don't want to do.

Once they recognized the various resistances that had kept them chronically late and impatient, Laura and Phil were able to break through the Achilles Syndrome. Instead of warring over lateness versus impatience, they saw that who they were and their love for each other were bigger than their respective Achilles Heels. Over a period of months, Phil was able to become more flexible and spontaneous. Rather than seeing his changes as "giving in," he recognized that becoming less impatient was helping him to be less tense and rushed. Laura became more aware of setting aside enough time to avoid rushing frantically to make appointments. Instead of feeling that her changes were "giving in," she was doing it for her own peace of mind. Now that they were no longer resisting each other's Achilles Heels, Phil and Laura could grow stronger together.

Mother's Work Is Never Done

Time pressures grow worse when we don't allow time for ourselves, time for relaxation and fun. Sometimes this happens when we don't fully value ourselves or the work we do. Today, more than ever, many mothers feel taken for granted, unappreciated, and burnt out. They feel overworked and undervalued, trying to be their mother's daughter, their husband's wife, and their children's mother. Some wait to be magically rescued, while others remain sullen and stressed.

Victoria is a thirty-seven-year-old mother of two who came for counseling because she felt "trapped." Victoria had been an account manager in the cosmetics industry until she married at thirty. When she and her husband decided to have children, Victoria recalls, "I had worked for almost ten years in some very demanding jobs and thought being a parent would be easy by contrast."

Coping with the demands of her new role was a lot more difficult than Victoria had imagined. Her first child was a baby girl who had severe teething problems and was colicky. Victoria recalled feeling alone and helpless. As she described, "Being a former businesswoman, I was great at finding a top obstetrician for doing ultrasound and amniocentesis, but what I was unprepared for is the time, devotion, and patience it takes to raise a child."

After the birth of her second child, a baby boy, Victoria had even more than she could handle. She explained, "Keeping up with a six-year-old plus a one-year-old is almost impossible. I don't know how women do it. I try sharing my frustrations with my husband, but from his point of view the kids are bundles of love he plays with after work. My mother is no help; she just says she had it worse."

Victoria felt overwhelmed by the seven-days-a-week, twenty-four-hours on-call responsibility of raising children. Underneath her constant feeling of being tense and rushed was a significant loss of self-esteem. Among her deep frustrations were the following:

- "I feel guilty whenever I take time for myself or even think about going back to work."
- "I resent people judging me on how clean my floors

are, how well-behaved my kids are, or how much money my husband makes."

- "I feel resentful of the fact that my husband's job ends when he leaves the office and my job is non-stop."
- "I feel trapped spending day after day cooped up in the house with children who throw temper tantrums, break things, and expect me to pick up after them."
- "I feel inadequate and unsure of myself when there are mothers who find time even to bake pies and sew quilts."
- "I have constant interruptions. I have to check on the kids and the laundry in between getting plumbing estimates."
- "In my career in the cosmetics industry I got a lot of acknowledgment, a title, and even a raise. Now I get dirty diapers and no vacation."

Being a new parent myself, I empathized with Victoria. When you become a parent, you appreciate that child care is an extremely time-consuming and challenging profession. You see how much talent, skill, and effort it really takes. Indeed, it is the most important of all professions. But, whereas the business world or the professions are deemed challenging and creative, far too many people still consider parenting the same as staying home and doing nothing.

Household management and the raising of children are highly skilled professions that could be called "domestic engineer" or "director of child care and development." When we discussed this together, Victoria and I came up with the following list of talents and responsibilities for this multi-faceted profession:

- Preparing nutritious and tasty dishes
- Child guidance and counseling
- Preventing and nursing colds, flus, and illness
- Managing finances
- Negotiating with plumbers, car mechanics, and other service people
- Mediating child disputes
- Shopping for all the household's needs
- Reading stories and tutoring
- Planning, organizing, and supervising family activities
- Teaching, disciplining, and providing role models
- Washing dishes, floors, windows, walls, clothes, furnishings—and soiled children
- Doing the work of bookkeeper, accountant, purchasing agent, inventory manager, and chauffeur

Plus dozens of other tasks, on-call at any moment.

Victoria had difficulty standing up for her needs and managing her time because she hadn't really perceived how valuable she was. I told Victoria that unless she saw herself as talented, skillful, and worthwhile, she couldn't expect others to fully value her. She had to communicate to other people her worth and competence as a full-time parent; otherwise they would treat her as unskilled or unemployed.

It emerged that Victoria had been comparing herself with the impossible standard of a supermom who can do it all without ever growing weary or having any needs of her own. No wonder she felt tense and rushed! To begin appreciating her professional accomplishments, Victoria took my suggestion and made a list of her successes:

- "I have two healthy, intelligent, and lovable children."

- "I've learned hundreds of new skills, everything from diapering with one hand to juggling our bills."
- "I can repair a leaky faucet and a running toilet."
- "I love to read stories and sing lullabies to my children."
- "I have always wanted to run my own business, which as a mother I certainly do."
- "I used to be oblivious to saving money, but now I'm ingenious at cost-cutting on clothes, foods, and toys."
- "Most days I handle my pressures and responsibilities remarkably well."

Once Victoria saw herself as a highly skilled professional, she could better appreciate that she needed time to relax and unwind. She saw that the more she took care of herself, the more she could give to her family, and she was able to feel less guilty when she looked for ways to lighten her heavy load.

I have seen that unless mothers schedule specific times for relaxing activities, there will always be something more urgent. Taking care of your own needs is no easy task when you feel responsible for the needs of your family. Victoria set aside several hours a week for her leisure interests, which included aerobics, reading, and journal writing. She initiated a once-weekly mothers group to pool ideas and share resources. She found excellent baby-sitters and a day-care facility for the times she reserved for herself.

After several months of treating her work as housewife and mother more respectfully, Victoria noticed some significant changes: "Now that I've found time to unwind, I have become a lot more loving. I ask for my husband's assistance more assertively, and he comes through. With the children, I'm a lot less overwhelmed and much more playful. My internal motor is no longer on overdrive."

> ✎ *Unless you schedule specific times for relaxing activities, there will always be something more urgent.*

"I Can't Slow Down"

The Achilles Heel of feeling time-pressured is most dramatic in the workaholic. There are important differences between being a hard worker and being a workaholic. A hard worker sets challenging but realistic goals, takes one step at a time, and schedules in fun and relaxation. A workaholic is driven to attain unrealizable goals and never seems to have time to stop, slow down, or enjoy. Whereas a hard worker finds pleasure both working *and* relaxing, a workaholic is constantly driven to work, for no matter what he or she does it is never enough.

Most of a workaholic's waking hours are spent feeling tense and rushed. A workaholic feels on call twenty-four hours a day. He or she fails to set limits on how much of the day should be devoted to professional versus personal priorities, wants to do everything completely and all at once, is driven to complete unimportant as well as important tasks, is often frazzled by frequent interruptions. Workaholics may say, "I can't afford to slow down," but their bodies know they can't afford not to.

> ✗. *Workaholics may say, "I can't afford to slow down," but their bodies know they can't afford not to.*

Whether you work for someone else or are self-employed, the person who really decides whether your work will be rushed or pleasurable is you. Even if you are overloaded with work, you are the one who can schedule tasks and breaks to suit your needs. You will feel perpetually overwhelmed as long as you are run by guilt, excessive feelings of duty, or an inability to set priorities. When you are rushing to meet the high expectations of others, each task may seem like do-or-die. One mistake and you feel like a failure. On the other hand, if you arrange your work thoughtfully, with an eye to regular respites and rewards, you will be more productive in the long run.

> ✗. *Whether you work for someone else or are self-employed, the person who really decides whether your work will be rushed or pleasurable is you.*

Use the following list of questions to begin discovering why your work feels more tense and rushed than it needs to be:

1.   Picture yourself getting ready for work.

   a.   Do you already feel rushed and behind schedule?

   b.   Do you gobble down your food between making phone calls?

   c.   Are you already making notes to yourself and your secretary while in the bathroom?

2.   Picture yourself arriving at your desk.

   a.   Is your desk covered with a multitude of notes and distractions?

   b.   Does your "To Do" list have more items than you can handle?

   c.   Are your meetings always scheduled too closely together to handle new business or take a breather?

3.   Picture yourself at half past four.

   a.   Do you still have several "musts" to finish before you can go home?

   b.   Are there numerous "urgent" phone calls to return?

   c.   Are you repeatedly distracted from important priorities?

4.   Picture yourself on a weekend, holiday, or vacation.

   a.   Do you bring work along that competes with relaxing and having fun?

   b.   Do you resent loved ones asking for your time?

   c.   Are you agitated or restless when you think about returning to work?

The Workaholic Couple

Lynn and Craig's case illustrates the steps necessary to transform a workaholic personality. Lynn and Craig met on opposite sides of a multimillion-dollar products liability case. As the vice-president of public relations for the company being sued, Lynn was working a sixty-hour week to save her company's reputation. As litigating attorney, Craig felt that his reputation hinged on this case.

Though both Lynn and Craig were reluctant to become emotionally involved with an adversary, their initial attraction grew progressively stronger. After they negotiated a fair settlement, Lynn and Craig remained inseparable. A year later they were married. Yet after three years of what seemed like an ideal marriage, Lynn and Craig were in psychotherapy. In spite of their mutual successes and substantial incomes, they felt drained, and their marriage was suffering.

An annual physical exam revealed that Craig's cholesterol and blood pressure were well above normal. As he lamented, "Today I watched myself wolfing down lunch with a client screaming in my ear and two other calls on hold. In the middle of all this I was proofreading a memo and thinking about the argument Lynn and I had this morning. We even have to rush our fights!"

Lynn felt a similar frustration when she looked in the mirror each morning and noticed the dark circles under her eyes. The first woman in her family to attend college and the first female in several of the corporate positions she had attained, Lynn described her life this way: "I used to be enthusiastic. Now I can't even get my eyes open without two cups of coffee. I've got tensions where I didn't even know I had muscles. There never seems to be time for Craig and me to relax and enjoy life together. One workaholic in the family is bad, but two is disastrous."

In addition, Craig's fear of failure and internal pressure inhibited his sexual desire. As he described it, "When Lynn starts warming up like she wants to make love, I start to become anxious about getting an erection." Lynn interpreted Craig's response as rejection: "It's like a reflex. I can feel him freezing up, so what am I to think? I don't turn him on!"

The workaholic couple can gradually asphyxiate their sexual desire. Your sexuality cannot be isolated from your life in general. You can't expect to strain at work for twelve hours, then come home and be ready for relaxed love-making. Workaholics treat themselves like machines; when the sexual equipment doesn't cooperate, they experience frustration and self-contempt. The workaholic couple may spend less than thirty minutes a week in relaxed, intimate communing and then wonder why their marriage is failing.

The workaholic couple may spend less than thirty minutes a week in relaxed, intimate communing and then wonder why their marriage is failing.

In some cases people become workaholics to avoid problems in love and marriage. If you and your spouse are having difficulties, it's much easier to say you have to work late than to come home to arguments. Addiction to work may be an excuse for avoiding sexual intimacy. When you and your lover accept the myth that one or both of you must work late night after night, you don't have to face the sexual problem. The longer this behavior persists, the more difficult the condition is to correct, and the more likely it is that a crisis will erupt. Sexual tension can often be relieved simply by setting aside ample time for unpressured intimacy and sexual pleasuring.

The decision to let their career ambitions come first, second, and third on their list of priorities had taken a toll on both Lynn and Craig. They were enmeshed in the Achilles Syndrome. The Achilles Heel of always feeling tense and rushed is especially insidious for people like Lynn and Craig who have been lavishly praised and rewarded for doing much more than required. Yet raises and promotions alone were not enough.

The key for such highly motivated and success-oriented people as Lynn and Craig is not to pack it in and join a commune. Most successful people resist dealing with their Achilles Heel of feeling tense and rushed because they are stuck in either/or thinking: They fear they must either strain at work or else suffer miserable failure and boredom. Yet all growth is based on optimal cycles of rest and activity. We are most creative, efficient, and loving after a good rest. The biggest hazard to satisfaction and effectiveness is to become burnt out.

> ✕. *All growth is based on optimal cycles of rest and activity. The biggest hazard to satisfaction and effectiveness is to become burnt out.*

Doing Less to Accomplish More

Lynn and Craig needed to reexamine their time schedules in order to restore vitality to their lives and relationship. I recommended the following guidelines for doing less to accomplish more:

- *Most time-pressures are self-inflicted.* Go through the list of the demands on you and eliminate those you've needlessly created for yourself. Ask yourself the basic question: Do I *really* have to do this? Does this meeting I've called have to take place? If yes, is my presence necessary? Do I have to cook for the dinner party tomorrow or will my friends be just as happy if we send for something from a restaurant? Do I belong to too many organizations? Do I have too many subscriptions to concerts and ball games? Do I put things on my list that my husband and children can better do for themselves? Do I have more social obligations than I can enjoy?

- *Stop taking pride in how much you overwork.* Ask yourself throughout the day whether what you are doing is your biggest priority or just more "busy-ness." Rather than priding yourself on the number of hours you put in, use your creative ingenuity and plan wisely. In your domestic life as well as in your work, find the best assistance you can afford and delegate work *and* responsibility to improve your efficiency. Even a small thing like having your laundry done for you instead of devoting Saturday morning to it can leave you more time for pleasure and your family. Surrounding yourself with satisfied, productive, and self-motivated people will save your most precious resource—your time and energy.

- *Hard work alone is never enough; you must listen to your inner voice in order to develop your creativity.* When you are centered and not afraid of quiet reflection, you are less likely to run yourself ragged. Drive and hard work are necessary, but far more important are your creativity and enthusiasm. The most valuable work you do in your job may be done in as little as five minutes! A brilliant idea, a pivotal decision, a simple solution, a telephone call. In those five minutes you accomplish more than shuffling papers for twenty-four hours.

> ✎ *The most valuable work you do in your job may be done in as little as five minutes! A brilliant idea, a pivotal decision, a simple solution, a telephone call. In those five minutes you accomplish more than shuffling papers for twenty-four hours.*

- *Don't overschedule yourself.* Most of us have a tendency to take on a lot more in a given period of time than we can do. Too often we plan a project without allowing enough time for things to go wrong (as they often do). A more effective strategy is to create deadlines that allow an extra 30 percent of time for human error, delays, and unanticipated problems. If things go remarkably well, the worst that can happen is the pleasure of coming in ahead of schedule, with a little bonus of easy time.

· *Take satisfaction in saying no.* Sooner or later we all have to learn limits. We can't be all things to all people or try to do everything that comes along. We must choose what really matters to us, or else outside demands will shape our lives.

· *Schedule breaks with as much serious intention as you would keep a meeting with a top client.* Too often we let problems at work push everything else aside. Relaxed time with loved ones deserves a high priority. A life well lived is not spent only accumulating assets for tomorrow. Enjoying a leisurely walk in the park is as important as taking on another hurdle.

> ✗. *Create deadlines that allow an extra 30 percent of time for human error, delays, and unanticipated problems. If things go remarkably well, the worst that can happen is the pleasure of coming in ahead of schedule, with a little bonus of easy time.*

· *Become aware of your optimum rest/activity cycle.* Just as you have a unique personality, you have an optimum work and play cycle. Some people are at their best in the morning, whereas others have their most intense burst of energy and creativity late in the day. You may want to relegate routine matters to your low points while protecting yourself from phone calls and other interruptions during your prime time.

• *Take a sabbatical.* To some a sabbatical of a few months—between jobs or perhaps even going on leave—sounds risky, lazy, or irresponsible. Yet if you use a sabbatical for personal development, it can be not only rejuvenating but financially profitable. Carefully planned sabbaticals will enable you to have a series of life experiences that will give you much diversity, renewal, and opportunity.

• *An ounce of prevention is worth ten pounds of cure.* It's more efficient to reduce stress and strain as a preventive measure than to wait until you are burnt out. Similarly, it's far less costly to learn to pace yourself before you acquire a serious illness. Set aside time each day for rest and rejuvenation. You may want to take a walk, read, or just daydream. Transcendental Meditation (TM) twice daily plus physical exercise will place you in an optimal state of restful alertness.

• *Cultivate a friendly relationship with time.* Instead of viewing time as your enemy, begin to use it as a creative tool. Whenever you set a reasonable goal and meet it with time to spare, reward yourself with a kind word or a pat on the back. When you find creative ways to shorten your workload, delegate time-consuming activities, or eliminate unnecessary steps, you free up additional time for more enjoyable activities.

• *Remember that failure is a part of success.* Some people are tense and rushed because they are tyrannically driven by a fear of failure. Yet, the very best hitters only get three hits out of ten times at bat. To succeed, one must know how to fail.

• *Striving for success is just another game that is not to be taken too seriously.* No matter how talented and hardworking you may be, you can never win at every challenge. Your sense of humor is essential in order to combat frenzy and the feeling that you are on a never-ending treadmill. The ultimate sign of your success may be the ability to laugh, to enjoy the simple pleasures of daily living. Even when you are approaching a "big" deadline, remember that you are bigger than any job you perform or compensation you receive.

After years of being workaholics, changing old habits was not easy for Craig and Lynn. Craig had to eliminate many superfluous activities that reinforced his feelings of self-importance. He stopped writing so many memos and going to meetings that were unimportant. He made himself less accessible to so many phone callers and kept his conversations to a comfortable minimum. He stopped taking home any work that he knew would distract him from really unwinding and being with Lynn. Leaving his work on his desk made it easier to leave his problems at the office.

Lynn, too, found specific ways to feel less drained and more vital. For example, she stopped jogging to the point of exhaustion and started running at an easy pace that left her energized. As a result Lynn experienced a breakthrough: "Yesterday after about two miles I was in an easy stride when suddenly inside I felt absolutely still. My legs were moving and my breathing was deep, yet I had no sense of strain. The joy was indescribable." Lynn rediscovered she could be both deeply at rest and satisfied amidst dynamic activity.

Craig and Lynn began making enjoyment of each other a top priority. They took a TM course and meditate together daily. They bought season tickets for the ballet, go camping on weekends, and learned to give each other relaxing massage. As their life-style became more nurturing, they rediscovered both their playfulness and sexual intimacy.

6. *Making Peace With Doubts & Expectations: "I Wish I Could Be Happier"*

A*re you waiting for a particular goal or person to bring* you a greater sense of fulfillment? Even if you consider yourself a basically happy person, you may be convinced you can't really be satisfied until a particular wish comes true. Many people seem to be caught on an endless treadmill of "I'll be happy when . . ." Here is what I hear most often at my seminars. Check your own hopes and wishes on this list.

"I'll be happy when . . ."

- I find the right person
- I stop searching for the right person
- I get this job
- I quit this job
- I start my profession
- I retire

145

- I take a vacation
- I'm back home
- I get married
- I get divorced
- I have kids
- The kids are grown
- We move to the country
- We move to the city
- We own a large house with property
- We live more simply
- I get a raise
- I get another raise
- The guests arrive
- The guests go home
- We have a simultaneous orgasm
- We stop being preoccupied with orgasm
- I make my first million
- I make my second million
- I can exercise every day
- I don't have to exercise every day
- We move to California
- We leave California
- I find the right guru, workshop, or therapy
- I stop searching for the right guru, workshop, or therapy

After years of delayed fulfillment, "I'll be happy when..." becomes a nostalgic "I *was* happy when...." People imply, "I was the happiest person in the world before I "met you," "took this job," "moved here." A married person believes he or she was happier when single. A divorced person wishes he or she was still married. A rich and successful person claims to have been happier when struggling to get started. A retired person recollects being happier on the job. Many of us live the first half of our adult lives postponing satisfaction and the last half with regrets.

Fulfillment seems always to be just over the next hill. This might not be so bad if, once over the hill, you could enjoy yourself. Instead, yet another hill looms on the horizon, and lasting satisfaction remains elusive. Even if things are going well, a person with the Achilles Heel of "I'll be happy when..." or "I was happy when..." can always find another "when" to impede satisfaction. But the past is gone and the future isn't here yet; we live each moment in the eternal now.

> ✗ *Many of us live the first half of our adult lives postponing satisfaction and the last half with regrets. Fulfillment seems always to be just over the next hill.*

"I wish I could be happier" is the expression of a common Achilles Heel in which wishing overshadows satisfaction and becomes a way of life. When your energy is tied up in hoping, worrying, or regretting, you give up your vitality and the power to make your dreams come true. Wishing without mobilizing yourself keeps you perpetually dissatisfied.

Like wings on flypaper, you are once again stuck in the Achilles Syndrome. The more you resist choosing satisfaction amidst your present circumstances, the more your dissatisfaction persists. The more your dissatisfaction persists, the more likely you are to be discouraged and resort to the old reliables of wishing, hoping, and maybe. Choosing to be satisfied doesn't mean you become complacent or "settle for less." Rather, by choosing satisfaction you will have more energy and enthusiasm for your goals and challenges. Instead of resisting the circumstances of your life, learning to appreciate yourself and what you already have can be the strongest starting point for growth and improvement.

Chronically wishing you could be happier gets in the way of taking charge of your life. Even though it may be years since you depended on your parents or ex-spouse for your happiness, you may still be secretly wishing that a Sugar Daddy, Earth Mother, or Prince Charming will somehow come to your rescue. You may be waiting for someone else to make you happy and resenting that no one does.

> *Even though it may be years since you depended on your parents or ex-spouse for your happiness, you may still be secretly wishing that a Sugar Daddy, Earth Mother, or Prince Charming will somehow come to your rescue. You may be waiting for someone else to make you happy and resenting that no one does.*

"I Thought Loving You Would Make Me Happy"

The Achilles Heel "I wish I could be happier" can seriously damage the best of love relationships. It's easy to blame your discontent on your partner's shortcomings by inferring, "Life would be perfect if only he (or she) would get it together." If you're bored or moody, you may be expecting your partner to boost your spirits. If your partner is unhappy, you may worry that it's your fault. No matter what you and your partner do for each other, one or both of you is forever dissatisfied and fantasizing that the grass may be greener somewhere else.

The unspoken contract for many love relationships and marriages has been, "I'll be responsible for your happiness, and you be responsible for mine." While this may sound loving, no one can make you happy except you.

Wishing for your partner to make you happy is doubly frustrating. Not only do you fail to take responsibility for your own happiness, but trying to change your partner into a perfect Prince Charming or Earth Mother is futile. The more you try to change another person, the more likely he or she is to feel rejected and unloved, and therefore resistant to change.

> *The unspoken contract for many love relationships and marriages has been, "I'll be responsible for your happiness, and you be responsible for mine." While this may sound loving, no one can make you happy except you.*

Though we must each be responsible for our own happiness, sometimes we can't help wishing that the person we fall in love with will, like McDonald's, "do it all for you." When infatuated, even the most sensible person can be heard to say, "I've finally found the one who makes me happy."

When the romance and infatuation wear off, we feel once again dissatisfied and disappointed.

A quality love relationship is not made up of half-full partners trying to rescue each other and become whole by merging. Only when both partners are striving to be full and complete within themselves can love and happiness overflow.

Walter and Irene's case illustrates breaking through the pattern of "I'll be responsible for your happiness, and you be responsible for mine." Married for eight years, this couple had the trappings of a happy life, yet they sought therapy because they felt "frustrated and dissatisfied."

Walter had successfully made it through dental school only to feel stuck in the dental partnership he had joined. When he changed to an office on his own, he discovered that the glut of dentists in his area meant he had fewer clients and a more modest income than he had anticipated. While Walter and Irene thought buying their own home and having children would make them happy, their home was smaller than they had dreamed about, and they couldn't afford a lot of help with child care. "With these and other financial pressures," Walter lamented, "I wonder if working this hard is worth it."

After an initial therapy session, Walter came to see the game he was playing. Ever since high school he had been anticipating and idealizing the future. He expected great but unrealistic satisfactions with the achievement of each subsequent goal. At first getting his own car was what he wanted. Next it was getting accepted by the college of his choice. Then dental school graduation and marriage were supposed to bring the fulfillment he had longed for. Although each achievement brought fleeting enjoyment, Walter's basic dissatisfaction would inevitably return. A gnawing feeling of being trapped kept haunting him.

How does Irene see their situation? Seven years younger than Walter, Irene is a kind, bright woman who trained to become a dental hygienist but quit work to raise a family. As she relates, "It looks like a wonderful marriage, but the nice home, beautiful children, and travel all hide the emptiness between Walter and me. He works hard and comes home late; I spend my time caring for the house and chauffeuring the children. When we're alone, the silence is conspicuous."

Irene was also frequently engaged in thinking, "I'll be happy when . . ." and wishing she could be happier. In high school she dreamed about college. When she got there, finding a husband who was a professional seemed the key to a happy future. When marriage didn't fulfill all her dreams, she hoped children would fill the vacuum. Irene had expected their marriage would be easy, affluent, and fun.

Like many couples, Walter and Irene had hoped since they first fell in love that "loving you would make me happy." Somewhat tight and introverted, Walter expected that an outgoing and adventurous wife would make him a happier person. Like many hardworking people who devote their energy to succeeding, Walter hoped Irene would take charge of his personal life. Irene was to be responsible for making sure Walter kept in shape, was entertained, and felt good about himself and his accomplishments. With such an assumption, anytime he felt insecure, bored, or dissatisfied —guess whose fault it was.

Walter and Irene's contract "I'll be responsible for your happiness, and you be responsible for mine" extended into their sexual relations. Both obsessed about what the other thought of their sexual competence. If Irene didn't have an orgasm, Walter was sure it was his fault. He would "push and pressure" Irene into trying to have an orgasm for fear he would feel inadequate. When Walter had trouble with his erection, Irene was sure she was to blame. Even after eight years of marriage, they would nervously ask each other, "How was I?" yet felt defensive whenever suggestions were made. Sex for them was anxious, rushed, and a source of arguments. Their sex life reflected the Achilles Syndrome: The more each worried, the more each had something to worry about, and the worse their sex life became.

In perpetually wishing for an elusive happiness, Walter and Irene had set up several no-win situations in their marriage. Walter couldn't succeed as breadwinner as long as expectations for his income were unrealistically high. Irene couldn't win at making Walter happy as long as he abdicated responsibility for his emotional well-being. Neither could enjoy sex as long as pleasure depended on some future performance.

Choosing Satisfaction Now

As I explained to Walter and Irene, all growth is the integration of seemingly opposite values. There's no crime in setting ambitious goals or aiming high. However, they needed to work on appreciating themselves right now.

Instead of seeing your life as being either 100 percent happy or else completely disappointed, it's far more productive to see satisfaction on a 10–80–10 spectrum. Ten percent of the time life is spontaneously wonderful: An admirer gives you roses; your kids return from school with A's; the airline upgrades you from tourist to first-class on your trip to Europe; you are left a large sum in your Aunt Bertha's will. Another 10 percent of the time life is extremely difficult: You or someone you love has a serious illness; your house is hit by lightning; the company you work for starts laying off people; your investment in a "sure thing" goes bankrupt. Particularly in the remaining 80 percent of living, life is what you make it: It rains every day of your vacation, but you have a terrific time in spite of the weather; one of your parents acts like a martyr, but you can enjoy your family visit nonetheless; you had a terrible night's sleep, but you still manage to be alert and at your best the next day; your marriage, home, or job doesn't fit all your expectations, but you choose satisfaction instead.

For Walter and Irene, as for each of us, attitude makes a crucial difference for at least 80 percent of living. When you find yourself thinking "I'll be happy when...," you must learn to choose satisfaction now. Instead of romanticizing the past or idealizing the future, focus on enjoying the present. Appreciating each moment is the most precious quality of all.

You can feel good even when you have problems. Many people think anxiety, worry, and tension are unavoidable as long as they're struggling with a problem or decision. This belief undermines their ability to solve problems and needlessly prolongs distress. To some people this idea may seem revolutionary, but problems don't have to make you unhappy! Life will always have its share of difficulties, in the midst of which you can choose to be satisfied, loving, and healthy.

To some people this idea may seem revolutionary, but problems don't have to make you unhappy! Life will always have its share of difficulties, in the midst of which you can choose to be satisfied, loving, and healthy.

Choosing satisfaction means cultivating an "attitude of gratitude." What you direct your attention upon increases its role in your thinking and action. You can exhaust yourself complaining and worrying about why you can't be happy. Instead, focus your attention on appreciating the positive. I suggested to Walter and Irene that they begin to share some positive energy with each other every evening at dinner: "Three good things that happened today are . . ." In addition, I urged them to live more in the present. For example, they decided to shift their quest for happiness by balancing their inner and outer fulfillment. Instead of just endlessly redecorating their exterior lives—with new cars, furniture, and travel—they sought to discover and deepen their inner lives. They stopped going to so many cocktail parties and spent more evenings with their closest friends. They took a philosophy of religion class to reexamine some of the basic issues of human existence. On weekends they spent more time with their children enjoying nature walks in a nearby forest.

As they began enjoying their lives more, their sexual difficulties lessened. What each wanted was not to struggle for a simultaneous orgasm but rather to feel relaxed, loving, and appreciated. As they stopped worrying about sexual performance, they became more spontaneous, sensual, and responsive. Walter and Irene began to feel excited about their life and grateful to be sharing it together.

Overcoming Self-Doubt and Fear

Fear begets fear and self-doubt begets self-doubt: The Achilles Syndrome surrounding self-doubt and fear can be tenacious. Desiring, yet at the same time uncomfortable with, personal freedom, you walk around "wishing you could be happier." To overcome self-doubt and enjoy your-self confidently requires first identifying and then mastering your fears. The following are the most common fears under-mining personal fulfillment and happiness. See which you recognize in yourself or someone you love:

- *Fear of personal power.* When you take charge of your potentialities and talents, you begin to feel much better about yourself. Your enthusiasm, energy level, and self-confidence all increase dramatically. Yet for some people this feeling of power is unfamiliar and even uncomfortable. When you have been living according to a dreary routine, opening up to the tremendous freedom of choosing satisfaction can be frightening. But you can transform the Achilles Heel of "I wish I could be happier" to an opportunity to regain your power.

- *Fear of self-discovery.* Some people keep a tight lid on their inner life for fear of discovering something terrible about themselves. Supporting this belief may be parental or religious injunctions that self-esteem is conceit, pleasure is bad, and any enthusiasm is suspect. Many cling tightly to the status quo to find safety from themselves. Listen to the resistances peo-ple have to self-discovery and letting go:

  - "I'm afraid to open up. If I do, I won't stay in my marriage."
  - "If I were to make happiness a priority, I'd quit working, and then where would I be?"
  - "If you're happy, you stop striving; too much happiness is dangerous."
  - "If I don't control myself, the hateful person inside me will take over."

- "Too much pleasure isn't good for you. You lose your perspective on the suffering of others."
- "I don't have time for my own satisfaction. Other people need me."
- "To be a good person, you have to expect to suffer."

- *Fear of being disloyal.* Some people fear that if they are happy, others will resent them. How can you be satisfied and show enthusiasm when your parents, co-workers, or spouse are forever complaining about their health or feeling victimized? How dare you enjoy your life when others are suffering? Is it disrespectful to achieve and make more money than your parents did, or to enjoy sex more than your love partner does? Holding yourself back out of a misplaced sense of loyalty can keep you from achieving your goals. It can make you feel burnt out and resentful of the very people you would like to help. The more you enjoy your own life, the more you can share your gifts with others.

- *Fear of losing control.* Some people suppress their desires like a military dictator afraid of revolution. They have sexual fantasies they would like to explore but they are afraid to lose control. They won't take a sabbatical from work for fear they'd never return. At a party, they want to let go and enjoy more but fear appearing foolish or inviting gossip. They dream of being less rigid and less tightly controlled, yet fear they may "run wild."

> ⤴ *Some people suppress their desires like a military dictator afraid of revolution. They dream of being less rigid and less tightly controlled, yet fear they may "run wild."*

• *Fear of moving forward.* If you are prone to self-doubt, you may frantically search for reasons not to move forward. The more you resist making the best of the choices at hand, the more stuck and full of doubts you feel. For example, when you are afraid of committing yourself to a relationship, you can always find an eccentric habit, a minor shortcoming, or even an unattractive mole for which to reject your partner. When you resist taking a new job, you can always point to a missing fringe benefit, the lack of an office window, or a co-worker who reminds you of your ex-spouse as a reason for staying unemployed. For fear of making a "wrong" decision, some people remain stifled in a relationship or job they have clearly outgrown. While a transition period is often filled with fears and uncertainties, in life nothing stands still. Not making up your mind is still a decision. It promotes self-doubt and keeps you from moving forward.

Empowering Yourself

Robin's case demonstrates how overcoming self-doubt and fear can lead to a happier life. Thirty years old and married to a successful computer sales executive, Robin worked in advertising and public relations. She was also an avid jogger and taught aerobic dance at a YWCA. Robin sought therapy because she was unhappy about the direction of her life. As she described it, "I'm still not sure what I want to do." Robin wanted to do something in the helping professions and had applied to several schools of social work. She had postponed getting her master's degree, however, for fear this decision, too, would not be right.

Despite the praise and promotions she had received at her jobs, Robin feared making "another mistake." She felt immobilized by fears and self-doubt. When I asked her to list the insecurities that bothered her most, she wrote the following:

- "I worry that if I don't find the right job soon, it'll be too late."
- "I doubt I'll stick to one thing and worry I'll still flounder."
- "I feel less motivated and creative than many of my friends."
- "I'm too dependent on my husband's income."
- "I'm worried about settling for something I'll get bored with."
- "I'm afraid if I'm gone more, my husband might leave me for a younger, more attentive woman."

Self-doubt had been Robin's nemesis since she was a child. Her parents held high expectations for her, but would constantly second-guess her decisions. The combination of high hopes undermined by doubts and insecurities left Robin feeling frustrated and dissatisfied. I point out to her that a key to overcoming self-doubt and fear is learning to trust yourself. Breaking the habit of second-guessing your every move may be the most difficult habit you've ever had to break. It's normal to have some doubts about your choice of career; the challenge lies in not letting those doubts block your inspiration and commitment.

During her psychotherapy, I emphasized the following strategies for mastering self-doubt and fear:

- *You are bigger than your fears.* Feeling anxious, depressed, or upset is made worse by taking too seriously the inevitably accompanying fear. This self-negating doubt deserves no more attention than you pay to static on the radio. Firmly tell your doubts to "stop" or "go away" and turn your attention to something more self-affirming. For example, list ten specific things about yourself of which you are most proud. Include your talents, determination, friendships, physical skill, and goodwill. Put this list on your bedroom nightstand and review it daily for at least a week.

> ✗. A *key to overcoming self-doubt and fear is learning to trust yourself.*

- *Unlock your breathing.* Fear restricts your breathing. Every state of mind has a corresponding state of physiology. The more you can unlock your breathing, the more easily you can break through fear. Sit comfortably, loosen your clothes, and take some deep abdominal breaths. Slowly inhale, hold, and then exhale, each to the count of four. Breathe easily and pleasurably. After four or five breaths, doubts are more likely to disappear.

- *Trust your desires and opinions.* Experiment with following your inclinations and instincts more often. If the mood strikes you to try something new, go for it and enjoy the experience. When you shop for clothes, try some new style, without being limited by what you've "always" worn. Purchase what looks right for you without being swayed by the salesperson's tastes. When you have a heartfelt emotion or opinion, don't depend on your friend or spouse to corroborate your view. The more you trust your own values and preferences, the less you will have to defend yourself and argue. Other people are more likely to respect your decisions and feelings if you are confident about them yourself.

- *Stop measuring yourself against a prefabricated ideal.* When you were a child, it was appropriate to try to live up to the expectations of parents and teachers. It is no longer appropriate, however, to punish yourself for not living up to the expectations and images of others. When you put yourself down for not measuring up to someone else's standards, ask yourself, "Who am I trying to please?" It could be your mother, father, a sibling, spouse, or other significant figure. Learn to live by rules that make sense to you instead of by the dictates of others.

- *Renew your energy and vitality.* If you feel fragmented, off-center, or stuck, it's often valuable to take a break. Go running, meditate, or listen to music. Do anything pleasurable to renew your vitality. Under stress, there is a tendency to go over and over the things that are bothering you. Though it's impossible to keep all your fears from ever returning, once you learn how to take a break and recharge, destructive doubts won't persist for long.

· *See your life as an adventure.* Fear can be converted to excitement, a stimulus to break through your limitations. Rather than giving in to your fears, take reasonable risks in small but steady increments. For example, you might go camping for a weekend in preparation for a month-long trek through the Himalayas. You might take a public speaking course in preparation for a talk at your club or house of worship. With each small success, you build up more confidence toward greater challenges. Ask whether you're doing what you'd like to be doing if you only had five years to live. If the answer is no, start making changes now. Whether you have one year or fifty ahead of you, your life is too precious to waste.

· *Accept the fact that failure and vulnerability are essential to being alive.* Watching my one-year-old daughter take her first steps, I learned a powerful lesson: It's not how many times you fall but how many times you get back up. Each person learns to walk by first stumbling thousands of times. In life you must be willing to risk failure many times before you become accomplished at anything.

· *Eliminate the words* wish, hope, *and* maybe. *Wish, hope,* and *maybe* actually erode your self-confidence by encouraging doubt, fear, and hesitation. For example, instead of saying, "I hope things get better," substitute a plan of "What I can do to make it happen." Instead of "Maybe I'll find a job" or "Maybe our marriage will work," come up with the means to find a great job or improve your marriage.

Visualizing and Planning for Action

To empower Robin further, I suggested a two-part exercise of visualizing her dream and planning the concrete steps to make it happen. We each need to find the right dream for ourselves and then make the dream come true. Here is a method I've had success with:

Set aside twenty minutes of uninterrupted time to relax with your eyes closed in a comfortable chair. Have on hand a pad and pen or else a tape recorder. You could also have a friend listen to you, without interrupting, to take notes.

When you feel at ease, begin brainstorming what you would like to be doing in five years. Where are you on that date? What might you be doing when you arise? Where do you go to work? What are your job challenges and responsibilities? What is your work space like? What do you do for leisure activities and exercise? How do you feel about your lifestyle? What are the gratifications and liabilities?

Don't criticize or judge an image that comes to mind. Save your evaluation for later, when you will develop a plan of action. For now, no idea is too bizarre, too wild, or irrelevant. The purpose is not to be "right" but to imagine without judgment many alternatives. Any combination of alternatives and ideas should be explored. Rather than stopping your train of thought by analyzing or judging, let the images flow and describe each with editorializing.

After a period of time—at least a day—your task is now to describe your very best options. Whereas the previous part was a free-flowing visualization, this step is more consciously directed. Evaluate the list you made of what you want to be doing in five years. What specific things do you fully intend to be, do, and have in five years? Explore all your choices. Please note: When describing what you want to happen in five years, choose things that are realistic and likely rather than things you know for certain won't happen. Aim high but remain realistic; set yourself up to win. Combine similar ideas and eliminate the truly absurd and implausible.

Once you have fully described and written down realistic five-year goals, decide what you need to accomplish or learn within the next year to stay on that path. Then write down in specific detail what you must do within the next two months to make your dream come true. Finally, describe in detail what you will do next week and within twenty-four hours. Once the fire is lit, the sooner you can begin acting on your goals, the better.

After you have laid out your five-year, one-year, two-month, one-week, and daily goals, explore the specific skills, information, and experiences you will need to support your progress. Whom do you need to call? Where can you find assistance, encouragement, and advice? What steps must you accomplish first to reach the goals you have set?

This exercise can be used not only for making a career change, as Robin did, but for major decisions, including your financial planning, an elaborate vacation, or an important work project. Be sure to include both the visualization of your alternatives and the development of a specific plan of action. Many people perpetuate self-doubt by visualizing wonderful goals that they fail to achieve for lack of a concrete plan. It is valuable to visualize and to make written lists that serve as both commitments and reminders.

In doing this exercise, Robin discovered a strong desire somehow to integrate her experience working with large corporations and her personal interests in fitness and counseling. While initially she didn't know if this was possible, she decided to suspend judgment. Bouncing her ideas off friends and loved ones, and making several phone calls, she heard about a new graduate degree program at a local university to train corporate health and fitness professionals. With great enthusiasm Robin enrolled and thus began to put into action her five-year goal of working with corporations to improve the health and work life of their employees.

As with so many people, once Robin found something she really wanted that was also realistic, it became easier to commit herself to a long-range plan and set her goals. Her enthusiasm also made it easy to enlist her husband's support. Today Robin is completing her graduate work, already getting client referrals, and doing workshops on executive stress management for U.S. and foreign companies. She plans to integrate her corporate consultations with her husband's business travel.

I pointed out to Robin that even with a clear set of goals, doubts can and will arise; the good news is that they don't have to run you. When you stop resisting doubts and fears, they are much less likely to keep on persisting. As with any Achilles Heel, you may get occasional attacks of insecurity much as you get a cold or the flu. One of the satisfactions that come from committing yourself to your vision is that you won't be distracted by how you feel on any given day. Choose your path carefully and then commit yourself to being satisfied along the way.

As Robin described it, "I use the "Visualization and Planning-for-Action" exercise for my semester schedule, promoting my services, and preparing for a seminar. While I still have some insecurities, they no longer slow me down. It's exciting to do something 100 percent instead of being run by doubts. My husband loves to see me knowing what I want and following through. I'm more fun to be with because now I'm doing what I like."

Resolving a Crisis of Meaning and Purpose

At some point in your life you are almost certain to undergo a crisis of meaning and purpose. You may suffer gnawing doubts about the life course you have chosen. None of the beliefs or principles that have ordered your world and established your place in it will be immune to question. Your confidence in the value of success, marriage, and work will be severely shaken. You will be plagued by doubts about yourself and commitments you already have or are about to make.

A crisis of meaning and purpose may occur at any time, but it is most likely during periods of major change. Typical events that can precipitate a serious questioning of your values and direction are the following:

- Enrolling in or graduating from college
- Marriage, separation, or divorce
- Choosing to have a child, adjusting to the birth of a child
- Major professional success or failure
- Major change in financial status
- Death of a family member or close friend
- Serious personal illness or injury
- Loss of job, career change
- Children leaving home
- Retirement

These events and others like them force you to reappraise your answers to fundamental questions. What do you value? What do you find most satisfying and meaningful? If you've had a big success, why don't you feel joyful? How well are you living up to your own standards of excellence and integrity? What are your real abilities? Your happiness and well-being for years to come depend on whether or not you translate these difficult questions into answers you can live with.

Most of us are ill equipped to recognize or deal with such a challenge to our status quo. You might feel unfairly tested, asking, "Why is this happening to me?" or "What did I do to deserve this?" Indicative of the Achilles Syndrome, the more you resist or try to ignore a crisis of meaning and purpose, the more tenacious it gets. The unanswered questions spill into every other area of your life, keeping you awake at night.

Instead of putting up your defenses, facing a crisis of meaning and purpose can dramatically improve your life. Though your world may seem in turmoil, a deeper sense of understanding and inspiration can emerge. A crisis of meaning is not a breakdown but an opportunity for breaking through. Use your anxiety as energy to search for adventure and purpose.

> ⚡. A *crisis of meaning is not a breakdown but an opportunity for breaking through. Use your anxiety as energy to search for adventure and purpose.*

Richard's case illustrates the struggle we each face at one time or another in resolving a crisis of meaning and purpose. A divorced thirty-nine-year-old attorney, Richard recently became a managing partner in a prestigious firm with corporate clients from among the Fortune 500. Richard's father had struggled through law school part-time while supporting his family. His greatest wish was for both his sons to become successful lawyers. He was deeply disappointed when Richard's older brother heavily abused drugs and dropped out of college. After that, Richard felt impelled to study doubly hard to achieve academic success.

Just after graduation from Harvard Law School, Richard was stunned by the sudden death of his forty-eight-year-old father. He was determined to fulfill his father's dream of becoming a highly successful lawyer. Defending some of the largest corporations in multimillion-dollar lawsuits, Richard acquired a reputation for combining impeccable legal research with courtroom intimidation. At the same time his personal life was, as he put it, "A complete mess. I had been having an off-again, on-again romance for two years with a woman who worked for one of my corporate clients. Just when I thought it was time to get married, I was shocked to hear her tell me point-blank, 'Richard, I can't marry someone so out of touch with his feelings.'"

Richard began to suffer from painful headaches that did not respond to his doctor's prescriptions of Valium and aspirin with codeine. In addition, he increasingly felt plagued by frustration, self-doubt, and generalized muscle tension. Having reached his long-sought goal of becoming a managing partner, Richard began questioning the direction of his life. One of his firm's largest clients was embroiled in a controversial case that involved an alarmingly high incidence of illness allegedly due to their dumping toxic industrial chemicals at a site near a housing development. Faced with the prospect of once again defending a client in contradiction with his own deepest values, Richard felt his life had reached a crossroads. After medical tests for his headaches proved negative, Richard took a friend's advice and came for therapy.

Mired in the Achilles Syndrome, Richard's persistent physical symptoms reflected his emotional conflicts. Sometimes headaches are caused by metaphorically striking your head against an internal barrier you may be resisting. Instead of just trying to medicate away his headaches, Richard needed to ask himself what his headaches might be trying to tell him. What internal wall was he bumping his head against? What feelings or values was he resisting? What in his inner life was plaguing him and making him feel dissatisfied?

The Quest for Integrity

Richard's challenge was no longer a question of measuring up to his father's expectations; it was now a matter of discovering his own sense of purpose and satisfaction. For many people who have achieved success, the driving motivation is no longer "How do I make the most money or rise above my peers?" but "What gives them meaning to my life?"

One way to discover how to live with integrity is to examine the difference between how you present yourself to others and your true feelings. People who suppress their true self in favor of a false image or a false act report feeling phony, dishonest, controlled, superficial, plastic, or "always on display." They are constantly rehearsing what they are about to say and criticizing the falseness of what they just said. They also become increasingly resentful of those whom they try to impress.

If you have been compromising your values, you may find yourself using rationalizations such as "If I didn't do it, someone else would," "It's the only way to get ahead," or "You can't fight the system." Eventually you may become cut off from your emotions, defensive with friends and loved ones, and only half-hearted about your success. Tired of straining and pretending, you often wish you could be happier but are afraid to let down the facade.

✒ For many people who have achieved success, the driving motivation is no longer "How do I make the most money or rise above my peers?" but "What gives meaning to my life?"

In contrast, when you are inspired to live by your deepest values, you are more likely to be free, spontaneous, alive, natural, powerful, loving, and enthusiastic. Instead of feeling that everything is a burden or that everyone is judging you, your emotions lighten up and your work becomes more meaningful. When you strive to do your best at something you value, you stop worrying about how you compare with others. You are more likely to appreciate your own goodness and the goodness of others and to enjoy being acknowledged not just for what you do but for who you are. There is no greater opportunity than to commit to your highest vision and live your life heroically.

I am a psychiatrist who thinks we don't need to endlessly "shrink" our problems as much as "stretch" our capacities to make a difference in the quality of life for ourselves, our loved ones, and the world. I sometimes joke that I have discovered that the mind is the source of all mental illness! Often what is needed is to move away from the same self-centered mindset and commit to something more deeply meaningful and purposeful. A key to overcoming the Achilles Syndrome is to find something bigger than your problems to inspire and challenge you.

> *We don't need to endlessly "shrink" our problems as much as "stretch" our capacities. A key to overcoming the Achilles Syndrome is to find something bigger than your problems to inspire and challenge you.*

Learning From What Ails You

I asked Richard to consider what his headaches might be telling him. After a few minutes with his eyes closed, Richard realized, "It feels like I've been way out of balance, overusing my head and neglecting my heart and spirit." Richard's alienation from his work had been stirring beneath the surface for many years. He realized that unless he made a major change in his career, he would remain emotionally blocked and unfulfilled. He also feared that if he didn't pay attention to his body's rebellion, he might wind up like his father and die at a young age.

Like many who contemplate a career change, Richard was terrified that if he tampered with the facade of success, the entire structure of his life would crumble. Often underlying the Achilles Heel "I wish I could be happier" is a fear that any change away from the familiar will wreck whatever small satisfaction we have. Richard worried that if he stopped working for a high-powered law firm, he would be ostracized and would have to start all over in a less rewarding career. He imagined losing his affluent lifestyle and facing all sorts of hardships.

I asked him to do the "Visualizing and Planning-for-Action" exercise described on page 162. In addition, I asked him to list the skills, talents, and experiences that would be his assets in any new career. Regardless of our training or profession, each of us has acquired, through direct experience, a variety of skills and resources we may take for granted or fail to acknowledge. Letting go of a self-destructive job, relationship, or habit is never easy, especially when you are unsure of what might follow. By focusing on the skills, contacts, and insights you already have, you make your chances for satisfaction and success much greater.

Richard was instructed to make a list of statements about himself, his career, and his experiences that started with the words "I can," "I know," "I have," or "I am able." After much deliberation, Richard included the following:

Skills

- "I can quickly sort through voluminous facts and issues to make difficult decisions."
- "I am able to see ways to do things more efficiently and thus prevent future litigation."
- "I have numerous contacts and information access in major corporations and the legal system."
- "I know how to work hard, overcome obstacles, and motivate people."
- "I have strong expertise on environmental matters and the problems of toxic waste."

I also asked Richard to clarify his values for a new career. Rather than fluctuating from one extreme of dissatisfaction—representing legal and ethical positions that he opposed—to another extreme of unhappiness—impoverishing himself and floundering—Richard needed to incorporate his values into what he chose next. He was instructed to make a list of "I want" statements to see what his values and priorities were. His list included the following:

Values

- "I want my new occupation to reward me emotionally and intellectually as much as it rewards me financially."
- "I want to be working with people who care about the environment and human issues rather than just numbers, company politics, and billable hours."
- "I want to be my own boss."
- "I want to build on my current expertise rather than completely starting over."
- "I want a quality love relationship and family."

Richard then used "Visualizing and Planning-for-Action" to find means for combining his skills and values. I told him he would experience a "click," a creative "aha!" when the right course of action presented itself. I reminded him to enjoy the process rather than feeling burdened by the need to make a decision. Lying on the beach with a pad of paper and pen, Richard came up with the following: He would resign from his present position and, using his experience and contacts, found and direct an innovative legal consultation firm. The company would advise corporations, legislators, labor unions, and consumer groups on how to protect themselves against the hazards of toxic chemicals. By helping to prevent environmental problems before they occurred and to design innovative cleanup programs, Richard could enthusiastically integrate his skills and values.

As he described his career shift, "It was more than just changing from a huge law firm to beginning my own business. For the first time my work consistently contributes something to the betterment of people's lives. I'm taking a cut in salary but feeling much richer. Since leaving my law firm, I've opened up a whole new circle of friends and associates among people I had previously avoided because they were 'the opposition.' Now instead of being 'us' against 'them,' my goal is to develop teamwork among corporate, scientific, labor, and consumer interests. I'm a lot more relaxed and ready to develop a quality love relationship. I want to share my happiness."

Where Do You Go From Here?

You have the power to create your life according to your personal vision; stop thinking of yourself as fragile. Behind every Achilles Heel is the fear of falling apart if you make a significant change. This belief is a self-fulfilling prophecy that can keep you absolutely paralyzed. The only way to break through this fear is to put your psychological strengths to the test. You will only realize how strong you are when you stop putting up with a destructive Achilles Heel and take specific steps toward change. It may not be easy, but you won't fall apart. Developing your psychological strength is just like developing physical abilities. The more you exercise, the stronger you become.

To get the most out of this book, review the principles and use them regularly. Be willing to experiment with some of the strategies that you may have at first resisted. You only have a nagging Achilles Heel to lose and a growing sense of power and satisfaction to gain. None of the techniques is difficult. All you need is a desire to grow and regular practice.

> ✗ *Developing your psychological strength is just like developing physical abilities. The more you exercise, the stronger you become.*

You will need patience and persistence as you work to make peace with yourself. Like Achilles, we sometimes forget that our birthright is not to be invincible but to learn, grow, and explore. This book contains tools for overcoming the most common barriers to your success and happiness. Whether the challenge is building a love relationship, appreciating your body, effectively handling criticism, reducing your time pressures, or choosing satisfaction, you can overcome the Achilles Syndrome and take full charge of your life.

While potentially there is a large number of Achilles Heels, you now possess strategies for dealing effectively with almost any psychological weakness or vulnerability. Knowing that there is no crime in having an Achilles Heel, you no longer need to deny, hide, or ignore it. You don't have to rush to fix it before someone discovers you're human. Nor do you need stubbornly to hold on to your Achilles Heel with the attitude "I'll never change. This is me, take it or leave it."

> ⤴ *Like Achilles, we sometimes forget that our birthright is not to be invincible but to learn, grow, and explore.*

Being more open with your loved ones helps to transform any Achilles Heel. Through intimate sharing, what you've been resisting in yourself can grow lighter. Here are several sentence completions to help you communicate more openly with loved ones about your Achilles Heels:

- "An Achilles Heel I no longer need to hide or deny is..."
- "A personal success I've never given myself credit for is..."
- "A self-destructive habit I'm ready to give up is..."
- "One of the ways I act defensive and shut down is..."
- "Something I want others to understand better about me is..."
- "Something I now understand and appreciate better about you is..."
- "A personal dream I am now ready to commit myself to is..."

The program I've presented challenges you to look at each vulnerability and "problem" in your life from a fresh and more positive perspective. What can you learn from an Achilles Heel that regularly trips you up? How can you make it less of a handicap and more of a stimulus to your personal growth? What skills and creative options can you pursue to transform this weakness into a source of strength?

The key to personal transformation is not to resist change but to enjoy it. Seeing yourself as a creative work-in-progress, you can feel enthusiastic that at each state of growth there is much at which to marvel. The same applies to how you view your loved ones and co-workers. The more you can enjoy the ever-present challenges to your continued growth, the more you can stop judging, resisting, or feeling put upon by the struggles and vulnerabilities of others. The more accepting of yourself you become, the more understanding you become of others. Making peace with yourself includes dealing with the faults of others as gently as with your own.

We can make a difference in the lives of others by confronting our own weak spots and insecurities. Many of history's most valued people developed a creative response to a painful Achilles Heel. Conflict and disability can stimulate our strengths as human beings. Human weaknesses need not be completely overcome in order to expand compassion and sensitivity for others.

As each of us learns to face up to our vulnerabilities, the barriers that keep us separate and afraid can start to fade. Instead of resisting the caring and understanding of family and loved ones, we can experience greater intimacy and trust. As we accept and appreciate the vulnerabilities we all share as members of the human race, we can learn to lay down weapons of destruction and build bridges of cooperation instead. The great challenge of our times, both individually and collectively, is to avoid Achilles' mistake. Rather than trying to become invincible and thereby destroying ourselves, it is far more courageous to appreciate that we are vulnerable and in need of one another's love.

References

Bloomfield, Harold H. *How to Enjoy the Love of Your Life*. Garden City, N.Y.: Doubleday, 1979.

Bloomfield, Harold H., with Leonard Felder. *Making Peace With Your Parents*. New York: Random House, 1983.

Bloomfield, Harold H., and Robert B. Kory. *The Holistic Way to Health and Happiness*. New York: Simon and Schuster, 1978.

Bloomfield, Harold H., and Robert B. Kory. *Inner Joy: New Strategies for Adding More Pleasure to Your Life*. New York: Wyden, 1980.

Branden, Nathaniel. *The Disowned Self*. New York: Bantam, 1973.

Burka, Jane B., and Lenora M. Yuen. *Procrastination*. Reading, Mass.: Addison-Wesley, 1983.

Colgrove, Melba; Harold H. Bloomfield, and Peter McWilliams. *How to Survive the Loss of a Love*. New York: Bantam, 1977.

Fisher, Roger, and William Ury. *Getting to Yes*. New York: Penguin, 1983.

Friedman, Martha. *Overcoming the Fear of Success*. New York: Seaview, 1980.

Friedman, Meyer, and Ray H. Rosenman. *Type A Behavior and Your Heart*. New York: Fawcett, 1974.

Freudenberger, Herbert J., and Gail North. *Situational Anxiety*. New York: Carroll and Graf, 1982.

Hegarty, Christopher, and Philip Goldberg. *How to Manage Your Boss*. New York: Rawson Wade, 1981.

Lakein, Alan. *How to Get Control of Your Time and Your Life*. New York: New American Library, 1974.

Linden, Paula, and Susan Gross. *Taking Care of Mommy*. Garden City, N.Y.: Doubleday, 1983.

Melamed, Elissa. *Mirror, Mirror: The Terror of Not Being Young*. New York: Linden, 1983.

Millman, Marcia. *Such a Pretty Face: Being Fat in America*. New York: Berkley, 1980.

Paul, Jordan, and Margaret Paul. *Do I Have to Give Up Me to Be Loved by You?* Minneapolis: Compcare, 1983.

Witkin-Lanoil, Georgia. *The Female Stress Syndrome*. New York: Newmarket, 1984.

Acknowledgments

I wish to thank all from whom I have drawn ideas and inspiration, especially Norman Cousins, Werner Erhard, Elisabeth Kübler-Ross, Arnold Lazarus, Maharishi Mahesh Yogi, Abraham Maslow, Carl Rogers, and my clients at the North County Holistic Health Center in Del Mar, California.

Appreciation is given to Ken Blanchard, Iris Browning, Adelaide Bry, Suzanne Caldwell, Hedges and Deborah Capers, Terry Cole-Whitaker, Bobby Colomby, Carolyn Crowne, Teri Davis, Barbara DeAngelis, Ken and Karen Druck, Mel Eisman, Bill and Anita Fitelson, Mike and Donna Fletcher, Susana Gomez, Johnny Gray, Trudy Green, Michael Jakes and Nikki Winston, Natasha Josefowitz, Robert Kory, Evone Lespier, Alice March, Barnett Meltzer, Howard Milstein, Victor Moreno, Elizabeth Orr, Jordan and Margaret Paul, Peter Reiss, Lew Richfield, Jacquie Roberge, Ali, Sybil and Phyllis Rubottom, Janice and Craig Ruff, Carol Schneider, Karen Schweibish, Robin Siegal, Gay Swenson, Neil Van Steenbergen, Clifford and Carol Ward, Suzanne Wickham, Tom and Deborah Willard.

For her guidance I wish to thank Margaret McBride, and

for his suggestions and support I especially wish to acknowledge Spencer Johnson.

Most of all, this book was nurtured from the moment of its inception by an extremely gifted and generous editor, Charlotte Mayerson. Her openness, intelligence, and warm friendship were invaluable.

Leonard would like to give special thanks to Linda Schorin for her creativity, strength, and loving support, and to Martin and Ena Felder for their love and encouragement.

I would like to express my love and deep appreciation to my wife, Sirah Vettese, for her contributions, devotion, and patience.

About the Authors

Harold H. Bloomfield, M.D., is a Yale-trained psychiatrist and one of the leading psychological educators of our time. Dr. Bloomfield's first book, *TM: Discovering Inner Energy and Overcoming Stress*, was an international bestseller and on the *New York Times* list for over six months. Dr. Bloomfield's *How to Survive the Loss of a Love* and *How to Heal Depression* have become self-help classics. Dr. Bloomfield has been at the forefront of many important self-help movements worldwide for twenty-five years. His other works, *Making Peace with Your Parents, Making Peace with Yourself, Lifemates*, and *Making Peace in Your Stepfamily*, introduced personal, marital, and family peacemaking to millions of people. Dr. Bloomfield's books have sold over six million copies and have been translated into twenty-four languages. His newest books are *The Power of 5, How to Be Safe in an Unsafe World*, and *Transcending*.

Dr. Bloomfield has appeared on "The Oprah Winfrey Show," "Donahue," "Sally Jessy Raphael," "Larry King Live," "Geraldo," "Good Morning America," and "Leeza," as well as FOX, CNN, and ABC News specials. In addition to professional journals, his work and popular articles have appeared in *USA Today, Los Angeles Times, San Francisco Examiner, Newsweek, Cosmopolitan, Ladies' Home Journal, New Woman, American Health*, and *Prevention*.

Dr. Bloomfield has received the *Medical Self-Care* Magazine Book of the Year Award, the Golden Apple Award for Outstanding Psychological Educator, and the American Holistic Health Association's Lifetime Achievement Award. He is an adjunct professor of psychology at the Union Graduate School and a member of the American Psychiatric Association and the San Diego Psychiatric Society.

Dr. Bloomfield is a much admired keynote speaker for public programs, corporate meetings, and professional conferences. He maintains a private practice of psychiatry, psychotherapy, and personal consulting in Del Mar, California.

For further information regarding consultations, lectures, and seminars, please contact: Harold Bloomfield, M.D., 1337 Camino Del Mar, Del Mar, California 92014, Office: (619) 481-9950.

Leonard Felder, Ph.D., is a licensed psychologist in private practice in West Los Angeles whose six books have sold over 850,000 copies and been translated into eleven languages. His books include *Making Peace with Yourself, A Fresh Start, When a Loved One Is Ill, Does Someone at Work Treat You Badly,* and the bestseller *Making Peace with Your Parents,* which won the 1985 Book of the Year Award from *Medical Self-Care* magazine. His newest book, *The Ten Challenges: Spiritual Lessons from the Ten Commandments for Creating Meaning, Growth and Richness Every Day of Your Life,* will be published in March 1997 by Harmony Books.

A widely requested speaker nationwide, he has appeared on "The Oprah Winfrey Show," "Sally Jessy Raphael," CNN, NBC News, and more than 150 radio and television programs and been invited to give lectures and workshops at colleges, churches, and synagogues in fifteen states. Dr. Felder is active in several volunteer activities and won the Distinguished Merit Citation of the National Conference of Christians and Jews for his many years of facilitating dialogues between people of different races and religions.

Originally from Detroit, Michigan, he currently lives in Los Angeles with his wife, Linda Schorin, and their son, Steven.